Social choice

For Matthew and Rebecca
who make it all worth while

SOCIAL CHOICE

A framework for collective decisions and individual judgements

JOHN CRAVEN

Professor of Economics,
Dean of Social Sciences,
University of Kent at Canterbury

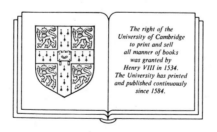

The right of the
University of Cambridge
to print and sell
all manner of books
was granted by
Henry VIII in 1534.
The University has printed
and published continuously
since 1584.

Cambridge University Press

Cambridge

New York   Port Chester

Melbourne   Sydney

Published by the Press Syndicate of the University of Cambridge
The Pitt Building, Trumpington Street, Cambridge CB2 1RP
40 West 20th Street, New York, NY 10011-4211, USA
10 Stamford Road, Oakleigh, Victoria 3166, Australia

© Cambridge University Press 1992

First published 1992

Printed in Great Britain at the University Press, Cambridge

British Library cataloguing in publication data
Craven, John 1949–
Social choice: a framework for collective decisions and
individual judgements.
1. Social choice
I. Title
302.13

Library of Congress cataloguing in publication data
Craven, John 1949–
Social choice: a framework for collective decisions and
individual judgements / John Craven.
p. cm.
Includes bibliographical references and index.
ISBN 0–521–32532–6 (hardback). – ISBN 0–521–31051–2 (paperback)
1. Social choice 2. Economics – Political aspects. 3. Political
science – Decision making. I. Title.
HB846.8.C73 1992
302′.13 – dc20

ISBN 0 521 32536 6 hardback
ISBN 0 521 31051 2 paperback

Contents

Preface

Social choice theory is a natural subject for an economist with a background in mathematics. I first discovered the theory as an undergraduate, and it was the subject of my first published paper. In twenty years of study, social choice theory has not ceased to fascinate me, but I have become aware that it has not had its due influence on politics, economics or philosophy. This book is an attempt to bring together its main themes, to provide a framework in which the theory can have a greater influence.

There are many related themes, beginning with the famous **impossibility theorem** of Arrow (perhaps it is this title that keeps social choice theory away from the centre of debate), through the work on strategic manipulation, theories of rights, justice and utilitarianism. All of these are introduced here: though we do not go to the frontiers of research in any of them. The main purpose of this book is to provide an integrated way of looking at the problems raised in social choice theory, and proofs of the main propositions so that they are reasonably accessible to readers without a formal mathematical training.

This book has been long in the making. I first thought of writing it when I was a visitor at the University of Guelph in Canada in 1982/3. Since then, I have been diverted into other things: studying the effects of the Channel Tunnel, which is almost in my back yard; being Dean of a large Social Sciences Faculty. Throughout this time, Cambridge University Press has waited patiently. While I was at Guelph, I had many interesting discussions with Clive Southey, and since my return to Canterbury, during the periods when I have found time to work on this manuscript, I have

welcomed thoughts and comments from my colleagues. John Peirson read
the entire typescript far more quickly than I wrote it, and his comments
on both style and content have been invaluable. Maurice Salles and an
anonymous referee read the typescript, and made many valuable
suggestions. My continued infelicities of style, errors and omissions are
entirely my own fault. During my time as Dean of Social Sciences, Lynne
Curran has guarded such time as I have for writing through her own
efficiency. To all these people, and no doubt to many others, thanks.

This book could not have been written without the support of Laura,
Matthew and Rebecca; what I know of practical democracy and justice,
I owe to them.

1

Introduction

1.1 Social choice theory

Social choice theory is a subject of very general application. It concerns the possibility of making a choice or a judgement that is in some way based on the views or preferences of a number of individuals, given that the views or preferences of different people may conflict with each other. This book provides both an introduction to and an overview of social choice theory. It is not a comprehensive survey of all the literature on the subject.

The problems addressed in this book have a common theme, but come with many variations. The central problem was demonstrated by Kenneth Arrow in his *Social Choice and Individual Values* (1951) where he showed that, if one imposes some apparently reasonable conditions on, for example, an election system, one finds that the system is undemocratic; indeed, one individual has dictatorial powers. Election systems are not the only contexts where this devastating result is important, and, in this chapter, we look at several other areas, including economic and moral contexts, in which social choice theory applies.

In chapters 2 and 3 we introduce the basic theory, first by establishing a formal framework for thinking about social choice, and then by showing Arrow's result itself. If Arrow's result were not true, we could then stop. However, given his result, we need to question much more closely whether the 'apparently reasonable conditions' are in fact dispensable. In doing this (chapters 4 to 6) we discover many other circumstances in which dictatorship is inevitable – in other words, Arrow's apparently reasonable conditions are not the only ones that lead into problems. We discover also that, even if we manage to avoid dictatorship, either some group has considerable powers, or we have sacrificed the ability to make the sort of definitive statements (such as which individual wins an election) that we are likely to want to make. We find instead that, at best, we can draw up a short list of possible winners, and then get no further.

As if these problems were not enough, social choice theorists have pointed out other difficulties (not entirely unrelated) where the desire to respect individuals' rights causes very considerable problems. We look at some of these in chapter 7. In chapters 8 and 9 we look at other aspects of social choice theory, most particularly when it is applied in a context of moral choice (rather than in an election or other area of applied social sciences). These chapters concern the possibility of views of justice where an individual tries to abstract from his own personal interests, and the possibility of using some form of measurable utility to make judgements.

As a subject of enquiry, social choice has attracted many of the most influential theoreticians in economics, political science and philosophy, and they have produced a range of important and challenging results. Yet it is not a subject that is fully accepted within any of these three disciplines: economists are suspicious of it to the extent that leading academic journals have contained views opposing the continued publication of so many papers on social choice theory. For example, the Report of the President of the Econometric Society in 1986 (*Econometrica* vol. 54, no. 2 pp. 447–53) indicated that a great majority of readers felt that there were too many papers on social choice theory. Also, in 1981, the editors of the *Review of Economic Studies* (vol. 48, page 1) indicated their intention to reduce the numbers of papers published on social choice theory. As far as I am aware, no other part of economics has suffered so great a reaction. Social choice theory has many interesting things to say about voting systems, including rival systems of proportional representation, yet some writers on these political issues seem unaware of some of the most basic conclusions of social choice theory. Social choice theory is intimately connected to philosophical discussions of moral judgements, but the issues raised by social choice theory are not always included in modern writings on ethics.

To some extent then, social choice theory is homeless; no academic discipline fully accepts it as its own. One possible reason for this (though surely not for many economists) is that much of the literature of social choice theory is presented in a mathematical form that many of its potential readers find terminally dissuasive. Significantly, this is rarely true of the central contributions, and need not be true of a survey such as this, as long as one does not mistake the use of logic and notational convenience for mathematical sophistication. We shall certainly use notations of various kinds, but, in the mainstream of the text, the logical arguments are sufficiently discursive to be accessible to those unused to the methods and conventions of mathematical set theory. We use simple examples, verbal arguments and tables to make our way through much of the theory. Chapters 4 and 6 have appendices which contain proofs of some results that are accessible with not much more mathematics, and are (as far as I know) not available elsewhere. Other results are beyond our scope, and their proofs are available in referred books and articles.

The range of social choice theory

Though we cannot apply a theory until we have developed it, it is useful to see the sorts of questions that social choice theory addresses, partly because these will furnish us with examples to illustrate the principles, and partly because a subject with no hint of context is dull indeed, except to those who take a pure mathematician's delight in abstract constructions for their own sake. So, for the rest of this introduction, we illustrate a variety of areas to which social choice theory can be applied, and to which we return in later chapters.

1.2 Elections

Many of the simplest illustrative examples arise from the problems of designing **electoral systems** and putting them into practice. An election for President, to Congress or to Parliament or for a less exalted status on a committee involves the combination of individual views of who should be elected into some sort of collective or social statement of who is elected – and that is precisely what social choice theory in general concerns. In an election, the individuals' views are expressed on the ballot paper or the voting machine, either as a vote given by each voter to a candidate, or as a listed order of preference. The electoral system defines the rules for combining these stated preferences to determine the winning candidate(s), and maybe also an order of first, second and so on.

For example, in a British General Election, there is an election in each constituency; each voter states his preference to the extent that he votes for one candidate. The electoral system (known as **first-past-the-post**) then determines the winner to be the candidate who has received the most votes; and, as a matter of psephological interest, but of no immediate practical importance, it also puts all the candidates in order by listing the number of votes for each. In some countries (Eire, for example) a system of **proportional representation** is used which allows voters to state not only their first choice, but also their second, third and so on. The electoral system may choose more than one 'winner' in each constituency – so that the constituency has more than one representative in Parliament – and in doing so takes into account at least some people's second and subsequent preferences. For a discussion of various electoral systems, see Newland (1982), Dummett (1984).

In electoral applications of social choice theory a number of important considerations arise. First, we can think of features of an electoral system; that many people would want to see. For example, it should treat all candidates equally, so that none has a built-in advantage from the system used. Such an asymmetrical built-in advantage would occur for an incumbent if, for example, the system required that a challenger could oust an incumbent only by receiving 75 per cent of the votes. Second, the principle of 'one-person-one-vote' implies that every person's view should, in some way, count equally. This principle rules out the extreme cases where an election is automatically decided by the opinions of one individual or small group of people – and also rules out the possibility that some people's votes are weighted more heavily than others.

Another, less widely held view, is that, in a multi-party system, the representation of each party in the local, state or national legislature should be in proportion to the number of people who support that party. This is not the place to examine the merits of proportional representation, nor the various possible ways of approximating to it. For our purposes, we can think of proportional representation as another feature of the electoral system which we could add to the requirement of equal treatment of candidates and of voters.

A particularly important aspect of elections is the possibility of **tactical or strategic voting**: an individual decides that it is in his own best interest to vote for a candidate (or to express an order of preference) that is not his true preference. In the British General Election system, tactical voting is widespread. Suppose that, in a constituency, everyone believes that the final outcome will be a close race between, say, Conservative and Socialist candidates, and that there is little likelihood that the Green candidate will be elected. Then any Green supporter is likely to be tempted to vote for whichever of the Conservative or Labour candidates he dislikes less – so as to keep out the less preferred of the two. Such strategic voting is certainly not irrational nor, within the context of this electoral system, need we judge it to be wrong. However, it does raise the question of whether we might design an electoral system that gives people an incentive to vote according to their true preferences, so that the true extent of support for each party can be seen. A considerable part of the modern social choice literature is devoted to the question of designing such **non-manipulable** systems.

1.3 Committees

Committees also use voting to reach decisions (see Black 1958 for example), and structures of decision-making have evolved in which the final outcome is reached by a sequence of votes. For example, suppose that a member proposes a motion to change a club subscription from $10 to $12, and another member proposes that the new figure should instead be $15. The usual procedure is to regard the $15 proposal as an amendment to the $12 proposal, and to vote first on whether this amendment should be accepted. Whichever of $12 or $15 then has majority support is then put as the motion to be voted on as the alternative to the status quo of $10. So, if a majority prefer $12 to $15, and a majority prefer $10 to $12, the outcome is that the subscription remains at $10.

It is easy to see that, in a committee of three members, the outcome of this procedure may be $10, even though a majority prefer $15 to $10. Suppose that Tom prefers $10 to $12 to $15, Dick prefers $12 to $15 to $10 and Harry prefers $15 to $10 to $12. Dick proposes $12 rather than $10; Harry proposes that this is amended to $15. This amendment is lost by two votes to one because Tom and Dick both prefer $12 to $15. Then the proposal for $12 instead of $10 is voted on, but this is defeated by two votes to one, because Tom and Harry both prefer $10 to $12. The subscription remains at $10.

However, if there had been a vote between $15 and $10, the outcome would have been $15, again by two votes to one (Dick and Harry both prefer $15 to $10). If the procedure were to vote first on $15 against $10, and the winner of that against $12, then the outcome would be $12. The final outcome is not independent of the order in which the votes are taken. In chapter 4 we discuss problems involved in devising a procedure in which the outcome is independent of the order in which issues are taken. This three-person example, with three alternative outcomes, is the simplest version of the **voting paradox** (which has been known at least since the Marquis de Condorcet's *Essai sur l'Application de l'Analyse à la Probabilité des Décisions Rendues à la Pluralité des Voix* (1785); see also Nanson 1882) in which **majority voting** gives rise to a **voting cycle** in which each of the three alternatives is defeated by another of the three.

Note that, in this example also, an individual may have an incentive to vote tactically in a way that does not appear to be in line with his true preference: for example, when the vote is taken on the amendment ($15 versus $12), Dick could vote for $15, against his true preference, because he knows that $15 can beat $10 even though $12 cannot beat $10. So by voting other than in accordance with his true preferences, Dick can get the outcome $15, which he prefers to what he gets ($10) if he votes according to his true preferences.

1.4 Economic contexts

At first sight, there is little in common between an electoral system or committee procedure and the economy. However, the 'outcome' of the economy – the level and distribution of national income, the inflation rate, the production levels of various goods, hours worked, unemployment and so on are (in part at least) the result of the combination of people's preferences. Consumers' preferences help to determine what they want to buy and how long they want to work; producers' preferences determine what goods they want to make and what method they want to use to make these goods – and the interaction of these demands and supplies helps to determine prices, wages, employment and other aspects of the economic system. The outcome, and particularly the distribution of income, depends also on the resources that each person or family commands: the skills it can supply and the other assets that it possesses – what economists call the individuals' **endowments**. However, for given endowments and technology, the pattern of prices, wages, outputs, employment and so on depend on individuals' preferences, and so a market economic system is a mechanism for making a social choice – it determines a social outcome given the preferences that individuals express.

It is well established in economics that when demands and supplies are equal in a competitive market economy (without externalities or uncertainty), it is impossible to make any individual better off without making someone else worse off: the outcome is **efficient** or **Pareto Optimal** (see microeconomics textbooks, for example, Varian 1987). It is not possible to produce more of one thing without producing less of something else or using more resources. However, where someone has a monopoly power that allows them to influence prices or wages significantly, the social outcome may not be efficient – and, as in the electoral example, someone may be able to gain an advantage by stating an untrue preference. For example, an individual who wants to buy a house may pretend that he is not much interested in it, so that the seller reduces the price.

Economic policy

It is also well established in economics that very few potential government policies give a definite gain to everyone. Most policies give benefits to some people at the expense of others who must, for example, pay additional taxes or have a new road running past their houses. One tradition in economics postulates that 'the government' in the form of an 'ideal public official' must balance the gains and losses of the policy through, for example, cost-benefit analysis (see, for example, Pearce 1971). In general the ideal public official must take account of individuals' preferences in choosing between policy options on behalf of everyone. There are, of course, some well-known problems involved in cost-benefit analysis: for example, it uses monetary evaluations of gains and losses and so presumes that one dollar's worth of gain is of similar social value whether it benefits a rich or a poor person. Also, any attempt to establish people's preferences, by, for example, asking them how much money would compensate them for some loss of amenity is likely to lead people to state untrue preferences. I may overstate the amount needed to compensate me for additional aircraft flights near my house as part of the evaluation of a new airport project. Such a false statement would increase the apparent social cost and so reduce the chance that the airport would be built (which is in line with my preference, but not necessarily in line with what would happen if everyone told the truth). Therefore I have an incentive to make a false statement and so manipulate the system to produce an outcome that I favour.

Within this tradition of welfare economics, social choice theory considers possible ways in which the ideal public official might make decisions on policy choice – taking into account individuals' preferences and the possibility that they might not tell the truth in answer to direct questions. However, the concept of an ideal public official is perhaps far-fetched; every individual is to some extent self-interested, and so no dispassionate person can exist. Even if such a person could be found, the economic system is so complex that many people are involved in implementing public policy, and the ideal official could not get all of them to act in a suitably dispassionate way. Then the main thrust of analysis must be to devise laws and conventions that lead to a desirable outcome, recognising that virtually all individuals are self-interested, and will not therefore do things only because they are socially desirable. One development of the theory of social choice (on incentives) considers the possibility of devising ways of using people's self-interest to achieve socially desirable outcomes.

This aspect of social choice (it still concerns the outcome that results from combining particular individual preferences) is directly descended from Adam Smith's *Wealth of Nations* (1776), which points out that the pursuit of self-interest in a free market system leads to a socially desirable outcome (in modern terminology, it is efficient or Pareto Optimal). Indeed, some writers believe that the principal objective of the economic and political systems is the extension of individual liberty, and so the government should restrict its activities as far as is consistent with the limitation of monopoly power and the preservation of law and order. For these writers, the economic system is not judged by its outcome at all, but by the method through which it operates.

1.5 Moral judgements

When we discuss the 'desirable' outcome from an election, or the 'best' form of social or economic policy, we are plainly making a personal judgement with which others, in principle, might not agree. Each person has his own interests – which may include his views about others' economic positions or their actions – and he may also have views about desirable policies or outcomes or about good actions that he recognises to be in conflict with his own personal interests. Thus there is no inconsistency in saying: 'higher taxes are against my personal interests, but I support higher taxes if the revenue is used to help the handicapped', or 'I disapprove of sexually explicit films but I accept that people should be able to choose whether or not they see them'. In each of these cases, the individual is making a distinction between his own **personal interests** and his **moral judgement** that is based on other people's positions also. Thus the process of making these sorts of judgements is an aspect of social choice – the individual is combining the preferences or interests of many individuals into an ethical statement.

In the example of taxes and the handicapped, the basis of the judgement is **sympathy** – a judgement of what it would be like to be in some other person's position. In the films example, the judgement is one of **rights** and

liberties, essentially of regarding another individual's freedom to do as he wants as more important than one's own desire to censor his actions. If the tax-benefit issue or the issue of censorship were to be put to a referendum, an individual would presumably vote according to his moral judgements and not according to his personal preferences. Thus the outcome of individuals' moral judgements (which may be based on his own and others' selfish interests) may in turn determine the preferences stated in an election that eventually determine what will be done – a two-stage problem of social choice.

Though an individual's moral judgements are likely to be based to some extent on others' preferences, it is unlikely that, in practical moral judgements, individuals weight all others' interests equally with their own. For example, there is likely to be a limit to someone's willingness to pay higher taxes to help the less well-off – and this limit comes before there is complete equality of incomes. However, moral philosophers have tended to concentrate on general issues, and upon how people can or should make their basic moral judgements. In these discussions, there is a frequent presumption of impersonality in that the individual making the judgement is expected to divorce himself entirely from personal considerations, and to do to others exactly as he would have them do to him (which we might translate into social choice terms as giving equal weight to others' interests as to one's own: a condition which parallels the requirement that everyone's vote is of equal importance in an electoral system). Alternatively, some argue that an ideal moral judgement between situations should be made as if one did not know which individual one would be. So, if we are judging whether to support financial help for handicapped people, the judgement should be made as if we did not know whether we would be handicapped or not.

Questions of sympathy, liberty and equality of moral judgements all come within social choice theory – as does the question of how we might compare the situations of different individuals. This last problem was raised in the great **utilitarian** moral tradition that continues to influence both philosophy and economics. In social choice theory, we discuss how we might measure and compare utilities – and, if we cannot measure them or compare them, how we might make comparisons without invoking utility at all.

Unlike an ideal public official, or a committee, a person making a moral judgement is assumed to have no influence over the actual outcome in any specific situation. Each individual is making his own moral judgement with no expectation of directly implementing it, though he may argue about it with others, or base his vote in an election on it. In the process of making moral judgements, no statement of untrue preferences (such as strategic voting) arises – in examining moral judgements we can take other people's preferences as given, although this begs the question of how we might find out what others want, or how they feel about certain issues.

The distinction between a personal interest and a moral judgement is not always easy to define. The simplest way would be to assert that an individual's personal interests are based purely on things that affect him. This is familiar ground to economists, who often assume that each person's preferences depend only on his own consumption of goods, saving and time spent working. We could take account of direct **externalities** (such as my pleasure in my neighbour's garden, or my displeasure in his barking dog) by defining my consumption to include my consumption of these goods or bads. But then I might be unhappy to pay taxes to build bombs, but happy to do so to help feed hungry people – even though my own disposable income is the same in the two cases. We can regard these as moral judgements of some kind, or say that, in determining my personal interests, I treat bombs as bads, and a reduction in the number of starving people as a good. However, this distinction need not detain us in that we can assess the process of making moral judgements by recognising that there are circumstances where an individual has conflicting opinions (higher disposable income versus helping the handicapped; distaste for some films versus support for freedom of choice) that must be reconciled in devising his moral views. The questions that social choice theory raises can be viewed as conflicts of which some are based on personal interests and some on moral principles.

Much of our argument in this book is theoretical – leavened by examples taken from the areas we have discussed in this chapter. Our concern is with the difficulties that arise when we put together even fairly simple restrictions on the social choices that arise from particular preferences. But first, in chapter two, we must discuss some aspects of the individual preferences that are the raw material of social choice theory.

1.6 Further reading

There is an immense literature on social choice theory: we do not refer to it all in this book – nor even to the greater part of it. In this section we list some of the main historical contributions and major surveys of the area, or parts of it, that have appeared more recently. In the remainder of the text, we acknowledge books and articles in which our main results first appeared or where proofs that we omit can be found. The reader who wants to look at everything available will miss little (except the most recent work) by looking at the bibliographies of the books and survey articles listed in this section and following the leads that they contain.

Arrow (1950) and (1951) is responsible for the growth of interest in the subject – and he refers to a number of earlier and contemporary writers (de Borda (1781), de Condorcet (1785), Dodgson (1876) – alias Lewis Carroll – Nanson (1882), Black (1948)). These forerunners were mainly concerned either with properties of specific electoral systems or committee procedures. The other set of forerunners to Arrow were concerned with more general problems in welfare economics that are not usually formulated in terms of social choice theory (Hicks (1939), Samuelson (1947), Bergson (1938), Kaldor (1939), Scitovsky (1941)). Arrow's own major contributions appear in collected form (1984).

Since Arrow's book, Sen (1970a) surveyed the field as it then was, and has more recently produced a number of survey articles (1976), (1977a), (1977b), (1979), which are collected together with a number of his most influential shorter contributions in Sen (1982). Those interested in the manipulability of choice rules (our chapter 5) will find the literature surveyed and extended in Pattanaik (1978). A fairly mathematical discussion of the work surveyed here is Suzumura (1983) who also has a substantial bibliography. Wriglesworth's (1985) prizewinning monograph covers the role of liberal (or libertarian) views in social choice theory in considerable depth.

A warning is in order: there is little consistency of notation or terminology in the literature – to the extent that different authors (or a single author in different papers) use the same term or symbol to describe different things. Acronyms abound also; these make papers shorter but often considerably less immediately comprehensible. A second warning is that much of the literature appears to be highly mathematical – a mathematical proof demonstrates that an argument can be made rigorously in a way that is not possible in a verbal argument – but even these arguments are often accessible to anyone who knows the basic notation of set theory and is prepared to read slowly.

2

Preference and choice

The examples of social choice theory put forward in the first chapter have one common central feature. Each example involves the combination of information about individuals' preferences into some sort of social statement. We begin this chapter with a discussion of individual preferences which establishes both the basic 'input' of social choice theories and a convenient notation in which to express it. Virtually every book on social choice theory introduces notation first – one of the hazards of the literature is that each author's notation is different. We stay fairly close to that of Arrow (1951).

2.1 Individuals and alternatives

In every problem that we examine, there is a set of n **individuals**, prosaically named 1 to n, and known collectively as the society. This society may be a whole community, some collection of electors, consumers or any other group of interest to us. In our illustrative examples, n is usually a fairly small number, though in reality an electorate may consist of millions of people.

The other 'raw material' of the theory is a set of **alternatives**. These are the things over which individuals have preferences, and could be, for example:

> candidates in an election
> proposals faced by a committee
> allocations of goods between individuals, so that each alternative consists of a list of the amounts of each good going to each individual

competing projects, such as airport sites or motorway routes
issues on which people are making moral judgements

In general, the alternatives are any situations about which some judgement or choice is to be made, and, from a formal point of view, it does not matter what these alternatives are. The term 'social state' is sometimes used instead of 'alternative' (though not in this book) to emphasise that the alternatives represent possible situations that the members of the society face. In this book we assume that the number of alternatives is finite. In principle, a set of alternatives would be infinite if they differ according to some continuous variable, such as a tax rate that could take on any value between zero and 100 per cent, but little is lost in most contexts by allowing a finite (but possibly large) number of alternatives.

Each of our n individuals holds a **preference** concerning the alternatives (for the moment we are unconcerned whether the alternatives are actually available to her). An individual states her preference in a simple way: faced with any two alternatives, a and b, individual i can say that:

she prefers a to b
she prefers b to a
she is indifferent between them
she wishes to make no statement between them

The terms 'prefer' and 'indifferent' are used in senses given in the *Oxford English Dictionary*:

Prefer (now the chief sense): to set or hold (one thing) before others in favour or esteem; to favour or esteem more; to choose or approve rather; to like better
Indifferent (definition 10): not differing in estimation or felt importance

Notice that this definition of prefer is strict: the thing preferred is definitely better than the others so that preference and indifference are mutually exclusive.

It is important to distinguish the third and fourth possible preference statements. The third is indifference in the sense defined above, whereas the fourth – that i makes no statement at all – involves indifference in another sense, as 'without interest or feeling, unconcerned, careless or apathetic'. We do not use 'indifference' in this sense in social choice theory – if we want to allow someone to make a statement of the fourth kind, we say that her preferences may be **incomplete**. However, most of social choice theory assumes that individuals' preferences are complete, so that they do not make a statement of the fourth kind. We make this assumption because social choice theory is concerned with combining individual preferences, which is a sensible thing to do only if people actually express preference or indifference as in one of the first three statements. So, in social choice theory, a statement of indifference between two alternatives implies that the individual has considered the alternatives, and has concluded that the relative advantages and disadvantages of the alternatives are exactly balanced.

In his discussion of individual preferences, Arrow (1951, p.17), whose book was the root from which modern social choice theory grew, states succinctly that:

It is simply assumed that the individual orders all social states by whatever standards he deems relevant.

Thus, for formal purposes we do not need to ask whether preferences reflect selfish interests or considered judgements. Obviously the nature of the preferences used and their interpretation depends on the context in which the theory is applied.

2.2 Preferences: notation and basic assumptions

Rather than writing (hundreds of times through this book) that individual i prefers alternative a to alternative b, we use the succinct and transparent notation aP_ib. Similarly, aI_ib means that individual i is indifferent between alternatives a and b. Finally, and slightly less transparently, aR_ib is used to imply that either i prefers a to b or that i is indifferent between a and b. Thus aR_ib if and only if either aP_ib or aI_ib.

In principle, an individual's preference can be described without the notations aI_ib and aP_ib. If we know that aI_ib, then, from the definitions above, both aR_ib and bR_ia, whereas if we know that aP_ib, then, from the definitions, aR_ib and it is not true that bR_ia, which is conveniently written as 'not(bR_ia)'. Conversely, if we know that aR_ib and bR_ia then aI_ib; if we know that aR_ib and not(bR_ia), then aP_ib. So individual i's preferences can be defined by statements involving R_i alone. For this reason, we shall use R_i as a shorthand way of referring to all of i's preferences about alternatives. So, in an example, we might say 'consider R_i and R_j...' which means 'consider the preferences of individuals i and j'. These preferences could be expressed using statements such as aR_ib, not(bR_ja), which can in turn be used to make statements involving P_i, I_i, P_j, I_j.

Individual i's preferences may differ or change between circumstances, and it is convenient to use R_i, R'_i, R''_i and so on to describe her preferences in each circumstance. Indifference in these circumstances is then described by I_i, I'_i, I''_i; strict preference by P_i, P'_i, P''_i and so on.

As we have seen, an individual could make the 'no opinion' statement so that none of aP_ib, bP_ia or aI_ib is true, that is neither aR_ib nor bR_ia. However, unless we specifically say otherwise, **each individual's preferences are assumed to be complete**, so that for any pair of alternatives a and b, she states one of aP_ib, aI_ib or bP_ia.

One final piece of useful notation. It is sometimes useful to talk about i's preferences concerning some but not all of the alternatives. The notation $R_i \mid T$ is a shorthand way of referring to i's preferences about the alternatives in the subset T. For example, the equation $R_i \mid T = R_j \mid T$ says that individuals i and j have identical preferences between each pair of alternatives in T, although they may have different preferences concerning some of the alternatives not in T (or between one alternative in T and one outside T). Likewise $R_i \mid T = R'_i \mid T$ implies that, when i's preferences change from R_i to R'_i, her preferences between each pair of alternatives in T do not change.

Transitivity

Each of the preference statements that we have considered so far (aP_ib, aI_ib, etc.) involves only two alternatives. If an individual is considering three or more alternatives, the question of the consistency of her preference statements arises. The most extensive form of consistency is **transitivity**: i's preferences are transitive if and only if all the following are true for any set of three alternatives, such as $\{a,b,c\}$:

if (aP_ib and bP_ic)	then aP_ic	(known as *PP* transitivity)
if (aI_ib and bI_ic)	then aI_ic	(*II* transitivity)
if (aP_ib and bI_ic)	then aP_ic	(*PI* transitivity)
if (aI_ib and bP_ic)	then aP_ic	(*IP* transitivity)

These statements are the 'common sense view' of the implication for the preference between a and c of preference statements between a and b and between b and c – and the labels (given by Sen 1969) at the right of the page refer to the order of the statements in the first brackets. If all statements satisfy *PP* and *II* transitivity, then it is easy to see that neither *IP* and *PI* can be contradicted. Suppose, for example, that *IP* is contradicted, so that aI_ib and bP_ic but not(aP_ic). Then:

if aI_ib and bP_ic then either aI_ic or cP_ia holds

if aI_ic then bP_ic contradicts II transitivity
if cP_ia, then aI_ib contradicts PP transitivity

So if IP does not hold, at least one of PP and II transitivity does not hold either. All four transitivity statements are implied by RR transitivity:

if $(aR_ib$ and $bR_ic)$ then aR_ic (RR transitivity)

For example, the following argument demonstrates that PP transitivity follows from RR transitivity:

start with aP_ib and bP_ic
these imply aR_ib and bR_ic
RR transitivity implies aR_ic
if it is also true that cR_ia, then, with bR_ic, RR transitivity implies bR_ia
bR_ia contradicts aP_ib which we assumed at the start
so it cannot be true that cR_ia
hence aP_ic as PP transitivity requires

In much of the literature of social choice, each individual is assumed to have complete and transitive preferences. Her preferences place the alternatives in order (though there may be ties in that order because she is indifferent), and we can refer to her **preference ordering**, her **most preferred** alternative(s) – which are those to which none is strictly preferred, and her **least preferred** alternative(s) – which are those strictly preferred to no other.

Note that, in some contexts, such as the analysis of some electoral systems, we do not need to know the individual's full preference ordering because, for example, she is asked to record only her first preference. Then it is not strictly necessary to know whether her preferences are transitive: i could vote for her most preferred alternative (Communist) if, for some unspecified reasons, her pairwise preference statements were:

Communist P_i Conservative
Conservative P_i Socialist
Communist P_i Liberal
Liberal P_i Conservative
Communist P_i Socialist
Socialist P_i Liberal

so that her preferences between Conservative, Liberal and Socialist are not transitive.

Where appropriate, we abbreviate the notation for preferences: for example aI_ibP_ic is equivalent to the three preference statements: aI_ib, aP_ic and bP_ic, and the notation aP_iothers implies that a is i's most preferred alternative. We devise similar notations where they are useful.

We frequently refer to a set of preferences, one for each individual. We refer to this set of preferences by (R_i), which is a convenient abbreviation for $(R_i \mid i = 1 \text{ to } n)$. If we want to describe preferences in more detail, we use tables such as table 2.1 in which the first column refers to the individuals, and the second records restrictions that their preferences must satisfy. There may be several transitive preferences that satisfy the restrictions given in a table: in the example, individual 3 could hold any of aP_3bP_3c, aP_3cP_3b, aP_3bI_3c.

2.3 Choice

Faced with a set of alternatives, an individual may be asked to choose one or more of them for some purpose. We say that $C_i(T)$ is individual i's **choice set** from T.

To find out an individual's preferences, we have asked the question (for each pair of alternatives) 'which of a or b do you prefer?'. If we were to ask instead 'which of a or b would you choose – assuming that these are the only two options available', we would have information on the individual's choices. Is it reasonable to assume that the answers to these two questions would be the same? Of course, if we allow indifference as an answer to the first question, we must allow that the answer to the second is 'I don't mind', or that her choice is random or arbitrary (based on things other than preferences, such as the alphabetical order of the alternatives' names). Allowing this, can we identify preference and choice? If we can, then we can deduce some preferences by observing what individuals choose and this gives some empirical information on preferences that is independent of the questionnaire method that we might otherwise use to find out preferences.

We must recognise the possibility that an individual's actual choice in a particular situation may be made for strategic reasons. We may observe a house-seller refuse an offer of $50,000 for her house and thus conclude that she prefers to have the house rather than $50,000. However, she may refuse the offer because she believes that she will get a better offer, although in fact she does prefer $50,000 to the house. We must be careful therefore to avoid the misleading influence of circumstances where some

Table 2.1 Examples of preference restrictions

individuals	restrictions on preferences
1	aP_1bI_1c
2	cP_2aP_2b
3	aP_3others
rest	aI_ibI_ic

possible choices are not currently available and the individual makes a strategic decision to wait for further opportunities to unfold.

In the absence of strategic considerations, we can formally identify preference and choice if people choose their most preferred alternative(s). In honour of one of the fathers of our subject, we call this principle the **Condorcet criterion**. This criterion states that the choice set from a set of alternatives is the most preferred alternative(s) in the set. In formal terms, i's choice set from T is:

$$C_i(T) = \{a \mid a \text{ in } T, aR_ib \text{ for all } b \text{ in } T\}$$

Note that this allows the individual to choose more than one alternative if several alternatives are preferred to all others. If real world circumstances are such that the individual is forced to choose a single alternative, she must do so using criteria other than her own preferences whenever she has more than one most preferred alternative.

When we consider only two alternatives, the identification of preference and choice using the Condorcet criterion is very straightforward. If i is faced with a choice between a and b, and prefers a to b then she chooses a; conversely, if we observe that she chooses a, then we conclude that she prefers a to b. If she is indifferent between a and b, then both a and b are in the choice set from $\{a, b\}$

It is always possible to derive preference statements from choices between pairs of alternatives simply by assuming that:

> i chooses some alternative from $\{a,b\}$
> if i chooses a alone from $\{a,b\}$, then aP_ib
> if i chooses both alternatives, then aI_ib

The usefulness of the Condorcet criterion depends on whether choices from larger sets are consistent with these choices from pairs. There are two reasons why this may not be so:

(i)   Choices may imply a cycle of preferences: for example $C_i(a,b) = \{a\}$, $C_i(b,c) = \{b\}$ and $C_i(a,c) = \{c\}$. If these choices were to be translated into preferences, we deduce aP_ib, bP_ic and cP_ia – which cause both a difficulty of interpretation (can these intransitive statements really be preferences?) and a problem with the Condorcet criterion because there is no most preferred alternative in $\{a,b,c\}$.

(ii)   Even without a cycle of preferences, choices could be inconsistent with the Condorcet criterion. Suppose that $C_i(a,b) = \{a\}$, $C_i(b,c) = \{b,c\}$, $C_i(a,c) = \{a\}$ and $C_i(a,b,c) = \{a,b\}$. The choices from pairs imply the transitive preferences aP_ibI_ic, but b is chosen from $\{a,b,c\}$ even though it is not a most preferred alternative.

Rational choice

We identified four aspects of transitive preferences, of which we can derive two (*IP* and *PI* transitivity) from the other two (*PP* and *II* transitivity). We speak of **rationality** rather than transitivity when we discuss the consistency of choices, but we can easily translate *PP* and *II* transitivity into **rationality conditions** that apply to choices:

RC1 if $C_i(a,b) = \{a\}$ and $C_i(b,c) = \{b\}$ then $C_i(a,c) = \{a\}$
RC2 if $C_i(a,b) = \{a,b\}$ and $C_i(b,c) = \{b,c\}$ then $C_i(a,c) = \{a,c\}$

Plainly, if preferences are derived from choices made from pairs of alternatives, and choices satisfy RC1, then the preferences are *PP* transitive; if choices satisfy RC2, preferences are *II* transitive. If choices satisfy both RC1 and RC2, then the derived preferences are *RR* transitive.

Conditions RC1 and RC2 may hold, but choices from larger sets may not be consistent with the Condorcet criterion and the preference derived from choices from pairs. For example suppose that RC1 holds and $C_i(a,b) = \{a\}$, $C_i(b,c) = \{b\}$, $C_i(a,c) = \{a\}$ but $C_i(a,b,c) = \{a,b\}$. Then we can derive transitive preferences aP_ib, bP_ic and aP_ic. These implied preferences and the Condorcet criterion would give $\{a\}$ as the choice set from $\{a,b,c\}$. So the stated $C_i(a,b,c)$ is not as the derived preferences imply.

Conversely, it is possible that choices are consistent with preferences derived from pairwise choices even if neither RC1 nor RC2 holds. The choice sets of table 2.2 illustrate this. RC1 does not hold for the three alternatives a, b and c; RC2 does not hold for the three alternatives a, c and d. However, choices from larger sets can be derived from the implied

Table 2.2 Choices not satisfying RC1

set	choice set	implied preference
$\{a,b\}$	$\{a\}$	aP_ib
$\{a,c\}$	$\{a,c\}$	aI_ic
$\{a,d\}$	$\{a\}$	aP_id
$\{b,c\}$	$\{b\}$	bP_ic
$\{b,d\}$	$\{b\}$	bP_id
$\{c,d\}$	$\{c,d\}$	cI_id
$\{a,b,c\}$	$\{a\}$	
$\{a,b,d\}$	$\{a\}$	
$\{a,c,d\}$	$\{a,c\}$	
$\{b,c,d\}$	$\{b\}$	
$\{a,b,c,d\}$	$\{a\}$	

preference statements using the Condorcet criterion. Therefore preferences and choices can be consistent with the Condorcet criterion even if neither RC1 nor RC2 holds.

The Condorcet criterion itself consists of two separable statements:

(i)   If i does not choose a from $\{a,b\}$, then the derived preferences imply bP_ia. Hence, using the Condorcet criterion, i would not choose a from any set T that also includes b. Put alternatively, if i chooses a from T which also contains b, then the Condorcet criterion implies that i chooses a from $\{a,b\}$.

(ii)   If i chooses a from T then the Condorcet criterion implies that aR_i(all others in T). If, in addition i chooses a from $\{a,b\}$ then aR_ib and hence i chooses a from the set $T \cup \{b\}$ consisting of the members of T together with b.

Expressed in terms of choice sets, these two statements become two more rationality conditions:

RC3 if a is in $C_i(T)$ and b is in T, then a is in $C_i(a,b)$
RC4 if a is in $C_i(a,b)$ and a is in $C_i(T)$ then a is in $C_i(T \cup \{b\})$

Note that RC3 is often known as rationality condition $\alpha 2$, and something very similar to RC4 is known as $\gamma 2$. We discuss these and other conditions further in chapter 4.

RC4 implies that we can build up the choice set from T from pairwise choices: if i chooses a from $\{a,b\}$ and from $\{a,c\}$, then she chooses a from

Table 2.3 Choice sets not satisfying Condorcet criterion

set	choice sets (I) RC3 satisfied RC4 not satisfied	choice sets (II) RC3 not satisfied RC4 satisfied
$\{a,b\}$	$\{a\}$	$\{b\}$
$\{a,c\}$	$\{a,c\}$	$\{a,c\}$
$\{b,c\}$	$\{b,c\}$	$\{b,c\}$
$\{a,b,c\}$	$\{c\}$	$\{a,b,c\}$

$\{a,b,c\}$. If, in addition, i chooses a from $\{a,d\}$, then she chooses a from $\{a,b,c,d\}$. And so on.

RC3 and RC4 are independent of one another: each can hold without the other, but, if one holds and the other does not, preferences and choices are not consistent with the Condorcet criterion. For example:

(i)   With the choice sets (I) of table 2.3, RC3 is satisfied, but RC4 is not, since a is chosen from $\{a,b\}$ and from $\{a,c\}$, but a is not chosen from $\{a,b,c\} = \{a,b\} \cup \{c\}$. The implied preferences are aP_ib, aI_ic, bI_ic which, if the Condorcet criterion held, would imply $C_i(a,b,c) = \{a,c\}$.

(ii)   With the choice sets (II) of table 2.3, RC4 is satisfied, but RC3 is not: a is chosen from $\{a,b,c\}$ but not from $\{a,b\}$. The implied preferences are aP_ib, aI_ic, bI_ic, which, if the Condorcet criterion held, would imply $C_i(a,b,c) = \{a,c\}$.

We might argue (and we shall generally assume) that individuals have fully transitive preferences, and that their choices can be derived from these preferences using the Condorcet criterion. In this case, we say that choices are **fully rational** and all of RC1 to RC4 hold, as do PP and II transitivity. However, it is very useful to isolate these various aspects of transitivity and rationality, because the assumption that society can have transitive preferences or make fully rational choices like those of an individual leads to many difficulties. These difficulties can be reduced to some extent if we do not insist on all aspects of the transitivity of social preferences or on all four conditions for fully rational social choices. So PP and II transitivity and the four rationality conditions RC1 to RC4 are very important when we come to analyse social choices (see chapter 4).

We have used the phrase 'fully rational' to describe choices that are consistent with transitive preferences using the Condorcet criterion, and this highlights the two aspects of rationality. First, rationality includes consistency, defined here by RC1 and RC2. Second, in everyday language, choices are regarded as rational if they coincide with the chooser's best interests – there is a maximising element of 'doing as well as possible'. By equating 'best interests' with 'preferences' we are making the liberal assumption that an individual is the sole judge of her own best interests. Without this liberal assumption we could argue that the preferences that are consistent with fully rational choices (that is, the transitive preferences derivable from choices from pairs of alternatives) do not represent the individual's best interest as regarded from outside. In some of our later chapters, we shall consider the possibility that individual i might judge the well-being of another individual j in a different manner from that revealed by j's own preferences, so that i argues that j's preferences are not identical with i's view of j's best interests.

Are preferences consistent?

It is possible to make direct tests of whether people's preferences are transitive – most simply by asking them, or somewhat more subtly, by observing whether their behaviour is suitably consistent. The latter requires that we observe an individual in a sequence of situations. In the first, a and b are available, and, if she chooses a, then we assume that her choice reveals a preference for a over b. In the second situation b and c are available, but not a, and, if she chooses b, she is assumed to prefer b to c. The transitivity of her preferences can then be observed in a choice between a and c; if she chooses a, she has revealed transitive preferences.

There is a number of possible explanations of observed behaviour that appears to be intransitive. First, inconsistencies might be explained by changes in preferences as time goes on. Second, the observation that i chooses a when a and b are available might not imply aP_ib; the preference may be aI_ib, and i has chosen a at random or according to some arbitrary rule because she is asked to choose one of the two. The observation that i chooses a from $\{a,b\}$, b from $\{b,c\}$ and c from $\{a,c\}$ is then consistent with the preferences aI_ibI_ic, which are transitive. The use of a random mechanism is likely to be revealed if i is faced with the same situation on several occasions – but the use of a non-random method to choose one from an indifferent pair would not.

A third possible way in which intransitivities might arise is that an individual's preferences as revealed by their choices may not be 'basic', because they are based on other more fundamental notions. If each alternative is defined by a number of items, such as quantities of different goods, or political candidates' attitudes to various issues, then it may be that an individual has preferences concerning each separate good or type of good, or each separate issue, and that she forms a 'composite' preference between alternatives by combining her various preferences concerning goods or issues. Then the individual's preference between, say election candidates, is itself the result of the aggregation of a variety of different considerations. Interestingly, this aggregation of one individual's views of various characteristics of the alternatives parallels the aggregation of different individuals' preferences about the alternatives that is the heart of social choice theory. We shall discuss circumstances in which social choices may not be fully rational, and this provides an argument for considering individual choices that are also not fully rational. However, we shall discover many problems of social choice that arise even when individual preferences are assumed to be fully transitive; these problems would be made worse if we were to extend the possible range of individual preferences to allow those that are not fully transitive also. For this reason – rather than some innate belief in the full rationality of every, or even any, human being – we presume that all individual preferences are fully transitive, and that individual choices are fully rational. We save our consideration of less-than-full rationality for our examination of social choices and preferences.

2.4 Preferences about sets of alternatives

In some contexts, it is insufficient to know only about preferences about pairs of alternatives. An electoral system, for example, may choose more than one candidate to represent a constituency, or a selection committee may make more than one job appointment. Then the voters or committee members must consider their preferences between sets of alternatives – perhaps on the basis of selecting a 'balanced ticket' or a representative group. We shall continue to use the same shorthand notation:

> UP_iT means that i prefers the set U of alternatives to the set T
> UI_iT means that i is indifferent between U and T
> UR_iT means that i prefers U to T or is indifferent between them

The statement UP_iT does not necessarily mean that i prefers each alternative in U to each alternative in T. For example, she may prefer a Socialist – Communist coalition to a Conservative – Liberal coalition even though she prefers the Liberal to the Communist, because she very strongly dislikes the Conservative.

It is plainly highly plausible to suppose that UP_iT if i prefers every alternative in U to every alternative in T. If, for example, $aP_ibI_icP_id$ then $\{a\}P_i\{b,c,d\}$. It is also plausible that UR_iT if the most preferred alternative in U is preferred to, indifferent to or identical to the most preferred alternative in T, and similarly for the second most preferred alternatives in each set, the third most preferred and so on (this supposes that U and T contain the same number of alternatives). Further it is likely that UP_iT if at least one of these comparisons involves a strict preference. So if $aP_ibI_icP_id$ then $\{a,b\}P_i\{c,d\}$, $\{a,b,c\}P_i\{b,c,d\}$, $\{a,b\}I_i\{a,c\}$, etc.

Other cases are less easy to assess: for example the preference between $\{a,d\}$ and $\{b,c\}$ when $aP_ibI_icP_id$. One assumption that is frequently used is the **maximin** hypothesis (we meet it again in chapters 5 and 8) that i prefers U to T if she prefers her least preferred alternative in U to her least preferred in T – she looks always at the 'worst' alternative in each set. So, if $aP_ibI_icP_id$, then $\{b,c\}P_i\{a,d\}$ because cP_id and $\{a,c\}P_i\{a,b,d\}$ for the same reason; the sets need not be the same size for maximin comparisons to be made.

This hypothesis can be extended to cases in which she is indifferent between the least preferred alternatives in the two sets (or it is the same in the two sets) by then examining her preference between the second-least preferred alternatives and so on: thus if $eP_iaP_ibI_icP_id$, then $\{b,d,e\}P_i\{a,c,d,e\}$ because the 'third worst' comparison is between e and a. The maximin hypothesis also assumes that i prefers some alternative to none: that is if $aP_ibI_icP_id$, then $\{a,b,d\}P_i\{c,d\}$: the maximin comparison is between a and no alternative, given that the least preferred alternatives are identical (d) and i is indifferent between second least preferred alternatives (b and c).

Preferences between sets of alternatives are also considered in traditional welfare economics, where it is assumed that an individual is made better off (has a higher level of welfare) if she moves to a situation that she prefers. Thus there is an implicit assumption that an individual's well-being can be described using her preferences – an assumption which rules out paternalistic views of what is good for the individual. In this welfare economics framework, an individual who is faced with a range of opportunities (limited, most likely, by her available budget and the prices of things she might want to buy) is assumed to buy the collection of goods that she most prefers from those available (her choice is determined by her preference). Then, she is made no worse off if goods that she does not buy are no longer available to her: if she chooses combination of goods x from the set T of available combinations, then she is indifferent between the situation in which she has T to choose from and that in which she is allocated x without choice. There is no welfare advantage or disadvantage in being allowed to choose: so $TI_i\{x\}$, and, in general, if i chooses x from T, y from U and if xP_iy then TP_iU. She judges any available set according to the alternative in it that she most prefers (and that she therefore chooses). This is a form of **maximax** assumption linking her preferences between single alternatives to her preferences between sets of alternatives.

In short, if we use a maximin assumption a set of alternatives is judged according to the worst thing in it; if we use a maximax assumption the set is judged according to the best thing in it.

2.5 Utility

Frequently in economics, and in ethics, individuals' preferences concerning alternatives have been expressed as **utilities** – and virtually every preference statement 'i prefers a to b' could be written as 'i gets more utility from a than from b' – with the qualification that i always prefers to have more utility than less. Similarly, 'i is indifferent between a and b' can be translated to 'i gets the same utility from a as from b'. We can translate from preference to utility (or vice versa) using the rules:

$$u_i(a) > u_i(b) \text{ is equivalent to } aP_ib$$
$$u_i(a) = u_i(b) \text{ is equivalent to } aI_ib$$

Making utility statements instead of preference statements is largely harmless – although there are three ways in which it can be argued that preference statements are superior – or at least safer.

First, there is a danger of reading too much into utility numbers used. If, on the scale we have chosen, $u_i(a) = 4$ and $u_i(b) = 2$ then aP_ib – but we may be tempted to ascribe meaning to the fact that $u_i(a)$ is twice $u_i(b)$, or to other purely arithmetical relationships between the utilities. Utilities that correspond to preference statements are entirely **ordinal** – i puts alternatives in order of preference or of greater and lesser utility; any meaning that might be given to the absolute sizes of utility numbers is **cardinal**, and goes beyond the usual meaning of preference. Cardinal utilities do have a role in social choice theory because they form the basis of utilitarian social choices, but we reserve further discussion until chapter 9.

Second, our discussion of the transitivity of preference statements implies at least the possibility that an individual may not always have transitive preferences. If we talk of utilities, transitivity must be taken for granted, since, if i gets more utility from a then from b, and more utility from b than from c, then i must get more utility from a than from c. Transitivity of utility statements follows because the arithmetic relation 'more than' is transitive. Similarly indifference statements must be transitive when phrased in terms of equal utility. Though this may not seem to be a great problem for individual preference or utility statements, we spend the whole of chapter 4 discussing circumstances in which 'social preferences' may not be II or even PP transitive.

The third reason why the use of preference statements is superior occurs only when there is an infinite number of alternatives, such as quantities of goods that can be of any size. There are then some circumstances in which it is possible to make transitive preference statements, but not translate them into any sort of numerical utility information. This arises when, for example, preferences are **lexicographic**: the individual judges alternatives on the basis of two or more quantities of goods x and y available to her. Alternative a contains quantities x^a and y^a, and alternative b contains x^b and y^b. If preferences are lexicographic, i judges alternatives first on the quantity of good x, using the quantity of good y only if the two alternatives have equal amounts of good x. So, aP_ib when:

$$x^a > x^b \text{ or } [x^a = x^b \text{ and } y^a > y^b]$$

The important feature of lexicographic preferences is that combinations of goods that are geometrically close are not 'close' in terms of preference. For example, describe an alternative by the amounts of goods involved, so that a is described by (x^a, y^a), etc.; if $x < 1$ and $y < 1$, then lexicographic preferences imply $(1,1)P_i(1,y)P_i(x,1)$. Then i's preferences put an infinity of alternatives between $(1,1)$ and $(x,1)$, because y can take on any value between 0 and 1, each of which describes a different alternative. This is true however close x is to 1. Thus even though $(1,1)$ and $(x,1)$ might be very close geometrically (x is very nearly 1), they are far apart in preferences. Put another way, i's preferences allow no trade-off between the two goods – no amount of the second good can compensate for the loss of a small amount of the first good; in economists' language, there are no indifference curves. If, as in the lexicographic example, points that are geometrically close are not close in terms of preference, it is not possible to assign utility numbers to correspond to preferences.

The name 'lexicographic' arises because dictionaries are constructed on the same basis: words appear in the order of their first letters; within those beginning in a, words appear according to their second letters, and so on. So, in a dictionary, the words 'bow' and 'tow' are many pages apart, but are 'close' in the sense that they differ in only one letter. We should note however, that the inability to ascribe utilities to represent preferences occurs only when there is an uncountable number of alternatives, as would occur if the two components x and y are quantities of goods available in any non-negative real amount. There is not, of course, an uncountable number of words in a dictionary.

The technical proof that we can assign utility numbers when preferences are **continuous**, so that points that are geometrically close are close in terms of preference, is of no great relevance to social choice theory (it is also technically difficult, see Debreu (1959); Sugden (1981) gives a diagrammatic exposition of the intuition behind continuous preferences). In this book, at least until chapter 9, we use the R_i notation for preferences rather than utility functions.

3

Arrow's theorem

3.1 Social choice rules

The central theme of social choice theory concerns the possibility of combining individuals' preferences to give a social choice from a set of alternatives. The simplest contexts to consider are where the social choice is to be implemented by some individual – a returning officer who announces the result of an election, an ideal public official who decides on areas of public policy – or where social choices are in fact the ethical statements of an individual who has taken into account the preferences of other individuals even though these may conflict with his own personal interests.

Throughout this book, we use the following definition. A **social choice rule** aggregates the preferences of all individuals to give a **social choice set** (consisting of one or more alternatives) from the set of alternatives, and from some or all of the subsets of the alternatives. So, for example, the method of determining from votes cast or preferences stated which candidate(s) win an election is a social choice rule.

In many contexts, it is useful to examine specific social choice rules (such as majority voting in committees; first-past-the-post). However, this case-by-case approach leads to the methodological difficulty that we might never exhaust the list of possible methods. This methodological problem is particularly important in social choice theory because there is, as we shall see, a sense in which every social choice rule has some undesirable feature – and so, by taking one at a time, we could face an unending search for one that was not undesirable or unreasonable in some way.

It would be reasonable to say that this case-by-case approach characterised social choice theory until Arrow's *Social Choice and Individual Values*. Arrow's main methodological innovation was to consider in one analysis all methods of making social choices that have certain properties by concentrating on the implications of these properties. We follow this methodology here.

In the literature, social choice rules come in various forms and under various titles. Arrow's starting point involves what he calls a **social welfare function**, which is a type of social choice rule. Essentially, Arrow asks whether it is possible to find a method, satisfying certain intuitively appealing conditions, that combines individuals' preferences – whatever they may be – to give full **collective rationality**. That is, the social choice rule must give social choices that look like the choices that a fully rational individual might make, so that they satisfy RC1 to RC4. Arrow's quest for a social welfare function has since been extended in various ways, and we shall use the term social choice rule to describe ways of combining individual preferences – even when these ways conform to all the requirements laid down by Arrow for a social welfare function.

As a notational convenience, we use the terminology $C(T)$ to denote the social choice set from a set T of alternatives, and $C(a,b)$ to denote the social choice set from the pair $\{a,b\}$. Where a social choice rule gives rise to fully rational social choices, we can talk about **social preferences** – which can be related to social choice sets using the Condorcet criterion that the choice set consists of the socially most preferred alternative(s). In parallel with the notation for individual preferences, we use P, I and R to denote strict social preference, social indifference and the combination of preference and indifference. Note, however, that the phrase 'society prefers a to b' begs the question (which we need not answer here) whether society is an entity that can meaningfully be said to prefer one alternative to another. In contrast, the phrase 'the social choice from $\{a,b\}$ is a' simply implies that some decision is made by aggregating individuals' preferences in a particular way. Questions of the legitimacy of the social choice process used still arise, but questions of the nature of society do not.

3.2 The domain of social choice

Two important conditions often required of a social choice rule are that:

(i)   It should define a non-empty social choice set from any subset of the set of all alternatives; that is, the social choice rule satisfies the condition of **choice from all subsets** or, equivalently, that there should be a **full agenda**.

(ii)   It should determine a social choice set from a set of alternatives for any combination of individual preferences (provided that these are complete and transitive); that is, the social choice rule satisfies the condition of **unrestricted preferences**, sometimes known as **unrestricted domain**.

In a voting context, the condition of choice from all subsets implies that the electoral system can define the winner(s) whoever the candidates may be (usually in an election, the actual candidates are determined by the nominating process and are a small subset of the potential candidates). The condition of unrestricted preferences implies that the electoral system defines the winner(s) however people vote (or whatever preferences they express). It would be unfortunate – no doubt undesirable, even un-democratic – if those operating an electoral system were forced to announce that the system had failed to give a result just because people had voted in a particular way. Similarly, in debates on desirable public policies and in committees, there is much to be said for announcing how a decision is to be made before the individuals' preferences are known – and for ensuring that the method used will work whatever preferences individuals may have (the rule may incorporate a prearranged way of breaking tied votes). Even in ethical discussions there is a presumption that the general ethical propositions that determine the relative merits of alternatives should be applicable to any set of individual preferences.

3.3 Independence

When a social choice is made from a subset of the alternatives, we can ask whether that choice should be affected by preferences about alternatives that are not in the subset. For example, most elections are held between a few nominated candidates. It is clearly much more efficient to have a voting system that uses only information on voters' preferences about the nominated candidates than a system that asks for their preferences about other potential, but not actual, candidates as well. This rules out, for example, the (perhaps bizarre) possibility that a Communist supporter who voted Conservative rather than Socialist (in the absence of a Communist candidate) should be told that his vote will not count because he is acting irrationally. His preference for a Communist should have no effect on the result of the vote between non-Communist candidates.

Table 3.1 Preferences showing that first-past-the-post violates
independence

	preferences consistent with	
individuals	I	II
1	bP_1cP_1a	$aP'_1bP'_1c$
2 – 10	aP_icP_ib	$cP'_ibP'_ia$

Similarly in a debate on a public policy decision, there may be many
potential alternatives (dozens of possible sites for an airport or a power
station) but only a few of these are under active consideration – in some
sense a short list has already been drawn up. The decision-making group
is likely (but perhaps not certain) to use only preferences about the short-
listed sites. In making moral judgements there may be a great many
possible actions, but the individual is attempting to decide his ethical
statement between just a few that are currently relevant. In deciding, say,
the circumstances that justify life imprisonment for homicide, one is
unlikely to take account of anyone's preferences about the appropriate
penalty for parking offences (perhaps – or perhaps not: if I knew someone
who would flog people who park cars in restricted areas, might I not then
ignore his views on the appropriate punishment for murder?).

To avoid having to consider all sorts of alternatives that may be thought
irrelevant to whatever is the subject of choice, we can make the
assumption of **independence**: the social choice from a set of alternatives
depends only on the individuals' preferences concerning alternatives in
that set. This assumption reduces, sometimes enormously, the amount of
information needed to make a social choice. Without this assumption, we
could not conduct an election without asking people their preferences
about every possible candidate – not just those who are actually
candidates in the election. In many circumstances, the independence
condition narrows down the social choice problem to manageable
proportions.

There is a more radical implication of the independence condition if the
social choice rule also satisfies the condition of choice from all subsets.
Then it must be possible to make a social choice from a set of just two
alternatives, and, if the independence condition holds, the social choice
from the pair must depend only on individuals' preferences about those

two alternatives. This condition of **pairwise independence** (also known as **independence of irrelevant alternatives**) is used by Arrow. To determine the social choice from {a,b}, we need to know only about individuals preferences between a and b; their preferences about other pairs of alternatives may change, but this will not affect the social choice from {a,b}. For future reference it is useful to note:

Theorem 3.1 A social choice rule that satisfies independence and choice from all subsets satisfies pairwise independence

The choices of a fully rational individual from all sets of alternatives can be derived from his choices from pairs of alternatives using the Condorcet criterion (equivalently, RC3 and RC4). Similarly, if social choices are rational and, if the social choice rule satisfies pairwise independence, we can derive social choices from all sets of alternatives from social choices from pairs of alternatives. The operation of the social choice process is much more straightforward in these circumstances.

As well as simplifying the derivation of social choices, pairwise independence rules out the use of any information relating to the strength or intensity of individuals' preferences. Suppose that, when one set of people very strongly prefer a to b, and another set just, but not strongly, prefer b to a (with the rest indifferent), the social choice is a. Then the social choice must remain a even if the preference of the first group for a over b becomes much less strong, and the members of the second group become very strongly in favour of b instead of a. The order of a and b in each individual's preference has not changed, and so the condition of pairwise independence permits no change in the social choice.

Majority voting satisfies pairwise independence because the choice from {a,b} depends only on the number of people who prefer a to b and the number who prefer b to a. However, a first-past-the-post election does not satisfy pairwise independence.

In the two sets of preferences in table 3.1, there is no change in individuals' preferences between b and c, but in column I first-past-the-post gives nine votes to a, one vote to b and no votes to c. The social choice from {b,c} is therefore b because b gets more votes than c. In column II, first-past-the-post gives nine votes to c, one vote to a and none to b so that the social choice from {b,c} is c. There is a change in the social choice from {b,c} even though there is no change in the order of individuals' preferences between b and c. Preferences concerning alternative a (specifically, whether or not a is anyone's most preferred alternative) affect the position of c relative to b and so first-past-the-post does not satisfy pairwise independence.

Independence and manipulation of preferences

Pairwise independence is a very powerful and important condition that has many implications, and it should be emphasised that it is the consequence of assuming both independence and choice from all subsets. If we drop the latter condition and require that the rule should be able to make choices from only some subsets of the available alternatives, then we need not use pairwise independence (see section 6.5). But, if we do not use pairwise independence, then the scope for individuals to gain by misrepresenting their preferences increases considerably. We have already seen in chapter 1 that first-past-the-post is manipulable in this way, and it turns out that this manipulability is closely related to the failure of pairwise independence. The intuitive reason is that pairwise independence ensures that the social choice from $\{a,b\}$ depends only on the individuals' preferences between a and b. So to alter the social choice from $\{a,b\}$ by misrepresentation the individual would have to say, for example, that he prefers a to b when he truly prefers b to a. With most reasonable social choice rules, a statement in favour of b over a would be likely to increase the chance that b is chosen instead of a, and so the false preference statement reduces the likelihood that the social choice is as the individual would want. Thus with pairwise independence, a false statement is unlikely to be of benefit. Without pairwise independence, an individual may be able to change the choice from $\{a,b\}$ by making untrue preference statements about his preferences involving other alternatives. We develop this theme of strategic misrepresentation in chapter 5.

3.4 Unanimity and the Pareto condition

The problems of social choice generally arise when people have different preferences, but we must not overlook the possibility (certainly allowed by the condition of unrestricted preferences) that everyone has the same preferences over all alternatives. If this is so, then it seems very reasonable that the social choice should be identical to every individual's choice. It is hard to argue against this principle of **unanimity** in any circumstance. Certainly in an electoral system, committee procedure or public policy situation, we would expect the social choice to mirror individual choices when there is complete unanimity. There might be some ethical circumstance when an individual wants to say that *b* is morally better than *a* even when everyone prefers *a* to *b*. However, even in these circumstances, the moral question that arises is the justification for not following a unanimous view – the question begins with the presumption that unanimity is a reasonable condition, and that departures from it must be argued very convincingly.

When the social choice rule satisfies pairwise independence, the unanimity condition leads to another condition that is very familiar at least to economists. If everyone has identical preferences over all alternatives, including a unanimous preference for *a* over *b*, the unanimity condition requires that *a* is the sole choice from {*a,b*}. Then, if individuals' preferences change (possibly in different ways), but with no change in the unanimous preference for *a* over *b*, pairwise independence requires that *a* should continue to be the sole choice from {*a,b*}. This is the **weak Pareto condition** that *a* is the sole choice from {*a,b*} if everyone prefers *a* to *b* whatever their other preferences may be. Note the difference between unanimity and weak Pareto: the former applies only when everyone agrees on all preferences; the latter applies whenever there is an agreed preference (not indifference) about a pair of alternatives.

For future reference:

Theorem 3.2 A social choice rule that satisfies pairwise independence and unanimity satisfies weak Pareto

Economists often use a somewhat more extensive version of the Pareto condition. The weak Pareto condition applies when everyone prefers *a* to *b*; the **strong Pareto condition** applies in more circumstances. This condition states that *a* is the sole choice from {*a,b*} if some individual prefers *a* to *b*, and no-one prefers *b* to *a*, though some people may be indifferent between *a* and *b*. This corresponds to what economists term a **Pareto improvement**, which occurs if someone is made better off and no-one is made worse off.

3.5 Dictatorship

We have so far discussed all but one of the conditions that we shall use in our version of Arrow's theorem: choice from all subsets, unrestricted preferences, independence, weak Pareto and the requirement of full collective rationality. When we prove Arrow's theorem, we shall see that these conditions are sufficient to demonstrate the inevitability of

dictatorship. The social choice from any set of alternatives is always one or more of the alternatives in the dictator's own choice set from those alternatives. If the dictator chooses one alternative from T, then the social choice from T is that alternative. If the dictator chooses more than one alternative from T, the social choice is some or all of those alternatives.

Dictatorship is, presumably, undesirable at least in any democratic context, and also in any caring moral theory where the position of one individual cannot be all-important. Indeed, in electoral applications, we are likely to want to ensure much more evenness of personal power than is implied merely by avoiding a dictatorship, but this requirement is irrelevant until we are sure of avoiding dictatorship.

3.6 Arrow's theorem

We are now in a position to show the following fundamental theorem which is based on Arrow's main **impossibility theorem** in *Social Choice and Individual Values*.

> **Theorem 3.3 There is a dictator if there are at least three alternatives and the social choice rule satisfies**
> > **choice from all subsets**
> > **unrestricted preferences**
> > **pairwise independence**
> > **weak Pareto**
>
> **and if social choices are fully rational (so that they satisfy rationality conditions RC1 to RC4)**

Note the requirement that there are at least three alternatives: majority voting between two alternatives satisfies all the conditions without giving a dictator. With three alternatives, some combinations of individual preferences give rise to a voting cycle with majority voting (see section 1.3) and hence to no social choice sets satisfying all of RC1 to RC4.

It is convenient to divide the proof of theorem 3.3 into several stages, to which we can refer in later chapters.

3.7 Proof of Arrow's theorem: the epidemic

We begin by demonstrating how Arrow's conditions spread decision-making power throughout the set of alternatives. Consider a set of individuals (not necessarily everyone in society) which is **semidecisive** for an alternative a over another alternative b. Set D of individuals is semidecisive if $C(a,b) = \{a\}$ when everyone in D prefers a to b and everyone else prefers b to a. Note that semidecisiveness occurs only when everyone not in D has the opposite preference over $\{a,b\}$ to members of D.

Table 3.2 Preferences demonstrating the epidemic of semidecisiveness

individuals	preferences consistent with		
	I	II	III
in D	aP_ibP_ic	dP_iaP_ib	bP_icP_ia
rest	bP_icP_ia	bP_idP_ia	cP_iaP_ib

Now consider preferences consistent with column I in table 3.2, where c is any other alternative. With the preferences shown, everyone in D prefers a to b and everyone not in D prefers b to a. If D is semidecisive for a over b, then $C(a,b) = \{a\}$. Everyone prefers b to c and so the weak Pareto condition implies $C(b,c) = \{b\}$. Then rationality condition RC1 implies that $C(a,c) = \{a\}$. But everyone in D prefers a to c; everyone else prefers c to a. So D is semidecisive for a over c (note that pairwise independence implies that a alone is chosen from $\{a,c\}$ whenever these preferences between a and c arise). We have therefore shown that, if D is semidecisive for a over b, then D is semidecisive for a over c and hence for a over any other alternative because c was chosen arbitrarily to be any alternative other than a or b.

Note that tables such as 3.2 state only the conditions that preferences satisfy; there may be other alternatives which may be in any position in any individual's preferences. Pairwise independence implies that preferences relating to these other alternatives are irrelevant to social choices from $\{a,b\}$, $\{a,c\}$ and $\{b,c\}$ in column I.

Now consider preferences consistent with column II in table 3.2, where d is any alternative other than a or b. D is semidecisive for a over b, and so $C(a,b) = \{a\}$; weak Pareto gives $C(d,a) = \{d\}$ and so RC1 gives $C(d,b) = \{d\}$. Examining the preferences, we see that D is semidecisive for d over b (note that pairwise independence implies that d alone is chosen from $\{d,b\}$ whenever these preferences between d and b arise).

We have started by assuming that D is semidecisive for a over b. From this, we have shown first (column I) that D is semidecisive for a over any

other alternative and second (column II) that D is semidecisive for any
alternative over b. Combining the second with the first, we have shown
that if D is semidecisive for a over b:

SD1 D is semidecisive for any alternative x over any other alternative
          y provided that D is semidecisive for a over y
SD2 D is semidecisive for any alternative x over any other alternative
          y provided that D is semidecisive for x over b

We can use these conclusions to demonstrate that, if D is semidecisive
for a over b, then D is semidecisive for any alternative over any other
alternative. For example, if the alternatives are a, b, c, d, e, ... then if D
is semidecisive for a over b:

SD3   using SD1, D is semidecisive for c, d, e, ... over b
SD4   using SD2, D is semidecisive for a over c, d, e ...
SD5   using SD1 and SD4, D is semidecisive for b, d, e, ... over c; for
          b, c, e, ... over d; for c, d, ... over e; for b, c, d, e over ...

The only remaining demonstration is that D is semidecisive for b over
a. This is shown using preferences consistent with column III of table 3.2.
SD4 implies that D is semidecisive for b over c, and so the preferences of
column III give $C(b,c) = \{b\}$. Everyone prefers c to a, so weak Pareto
gives $C(a,c) = \{c\}$. Then RC1 gives $C(a,b) = \{b\}$, and D is semidecisive for
b over a (note that pairwise independence implies that b alone is chosen
from $\{a,b\}$ whenever these preferences between a and b arise).

We began this part of the proof with the assumption that D is
semidecisive for a over b, and have shown that D is semidecisive for any
alternative over any other alternative: suffice to say that D is **semidecisive**.
The initial assumption has led to a spread or **epidemic** of semidecisiveness.

Decisiveness

Semidecisiveness is a curious kind of power, in that members of D
determine the social preference only when everyone else opposes. We have
not yet shown that D can enforce its choice from $\{a,b\}$ when some others
agree with members of D, or are indifferent. In a sense, we have
established the extreme case: D imposes its view when everyone else is
opposed, and so it seems likely that D can impose its preference in other
circumstances too. We can now demonstrate this by considering
preferences consistent with table 3.3, where c, d and e are any three

alternatives (including any of a or b from the previous part of the proof). D is semidecisive, and so $C(d,e) = \{d\}$. By weak Pareto $C(c,e) = \{e\}$, and so RC1 gives $C(c,d) = \{d\}$. The members of D can impose their choice whatever preferences others have over $\{c,d\}$ (those in E support those in D; those in F oppose; the rest are indifferent. These categories allow for any division of the people not in D and any number of people).

Table 3.3 Preferences demonstrating decisiveness

individuals	preferences consistent with
in D	$dP_i eP_i c$
in E	$eP_i dP_i c$
in F	$eP_i cP_i d$
rest	$eP_i cI_i d$

We then say that D is a **decisive** set of individuals: whenever the members of D agree on preference on a pair of alternatives (not indifference) then the social choice reflects that preference, whatever preferences others have. So we have shown how Arrow's conditions spread power from initial semidecisiveness involving two alternatives to decisiveness. Checking back through the argument we can confirm that we have so far used only RC1 of the four rationality conditions. Therefore:

Theorem 3.4 D is a decisive set if there are at least three alternatives, if D is semidecisive for a over b, if the social choice rule satisfies
    choice from all subsets
    unrestricted preferences
    pairwise independence
    weak Pareto
and if social choices satisfy rationality condition RC1

So far we have considered the influence of a set of individuals D on the choice from pairs of alternatives. Suppose now that everyone in a decisive set D agrees that a is the unique most preferred alternative in some set T. Then, for any other alternative b in T, everyone in D prefers a to b, and so the social choice $C(a,b) = \{a\}$. Now if b were in $C(T)$, RC3 implies that b would be in $C(a,b)$. So b cannot be in $C(T)$. This is true for any alternative in T other than a, and so $C(T) = \{a\}$. The social choice from

T is the same as that of the members of D. We say that a set of individuals with this sort of power is **fully decisive**: D can ensure that a is chosen whenever a is the most preferred alternative of all individuals in D. We have shown

> **Theorem 3.5 D is a fully decisive set if there are at least three alternatives, D is semidecisive for a over b, if the social choice rule satisfies**
> > **choice from all subsets**
> > **unrestricted preferences**
> > **pairwise independence**
> > **weak Pareto**
> **and if social choices satisfy rationality conditions RC1 and RC3**

Theorem 3.5 shows the full extent of the epidemic spread of power: a set of individuals who start as semidecisive for one alternative over another is fully decisive, assuming that the social choice rule satisfies the conditions stated in the theorem. All of the theorems hold for two or more people.

Welfarism

In electoral systems this epidemic is not likely to be a criticism, because in most circumstances we want equality of treatment for all candidates. If a group of voters is large enough to be able to ensure the election of a Liberal candidate (if they all agree he is the most preferred) when there is a choice between Liberal and Communist, then equality of treatment implies that the same group can ensure the election of a Socialist candidate if the choice is between Socialist and Conservative. Similar considerations may apply in committee decisions and in at least some choices of public policies, but there is certainly a difficulty with this epidemic in ethical judgements. The epidemic implies that the process of social choice is **welfarist** in the sense that the social choice is based entirely on individuals' preferences about the alternatives. There is no scope for deciding any issue on the basis of other information, such as the moral nature of the alternatives concerned, or individuals' rights in certain circumstances. Sen (1979) discusses welfarism in depth: he uses the term **strict ranking welfarism** to reflect the fact that the preferences involved in semi-decisiveness are all strict preferences.

In particular, the epidemic proposition tells us to beware of individual rights. To summarise the longer discussion in chapter 7, j has a right if he

is allowed by the social choice rule to determine the social choice from
{a,b}, presumably because the difference between a and b is some issue that
is entirely personal to him (perhaps like his choice of clothes, the issue
need not be one of great moment), whatever preferences others have. With
such a right, j is semidecisive for a over b, and so, given the other
conditions, he is fully decisive – indeed, he is a dictator. He can impose the
social choice in any circumstance where he has a strict preference.
Furthermore, there cannot be two dictators, so two people cannot have
rights if the social choice rule satisfies the conditions of theorem 3.5. The
radical implications of this paragraph are the theme of chapter 7.

3.8 Proof of Arrow's theorem: the collective

There is certainly one semidecisive set of individuals – society itself. If
everyone prefers a to b, then, by weak Pareto, a is the sole choice from
{a,b}. Society is a fully decisive set, and there may be smaller fully decisive
sets. Let D and E be two fully decisive sets which have members in
common (there cannot be two without members in common – what would
happen when their members disagree?), and consider preferences
consistent with the restrictions of table 3.4.

   Everyone in D prefers b to c, so $C(b,c) = \{b\}$; everyone in E prefers c
to a, so $C(a,c) = \{c\}$. By RC1, $C(a,b) = \{b\}$. Everyone who is in both D
and E prefers b to a; everyone else prefers a to b. So the individuals
common to D and E form a set that is semidecisive for b over a, and
hence, under the conditions of theorem 3.5, a fully decisive set. The
common members of any two fully decisive sets form a fully decisive set.

Table 3.4 Preferences of intersecting fully decisive sets

individuals	preferences consistent with
in D and in E	bP_icP_ia
in D, not in E	aP_ibP_ic
in E, not in D	cP_iaP_ib
rest	aP_icP_ib

This conclusion implies that we can find a fully decisive set (which we call D^*) which consists of the common members of all other fully decisive sets. All other fully decisive sets contain D^*, which is known as a **collective**. If all the members of the collective prefer a to b, then b cannot be chosen from any set which also contains a. If all the members of a collective agree on their uniquely most preferred alternative in some set, then that alternative is the sole social choice from that set, whatever preferences others may have.

The important features of a collective are:

(i)   a collective is the smallest fully decisive set,
(ii)   all sets that include all members of the collective are fully decisive,
(iii)   no set that does not include all members of the collective is fully decisive,
(iv)   there can only be one collective.

Note also that if all members of the collective are indifferent between all alternatives in a subset U of T, and prefer any alternative in U to all other alternatives in T, then $C(T)$ contains some, but not necessarily all, alternatives in U – and $C(T)$ contains no alternative not in U.

We have shown:

Theorem 3.6 There is a collective if there are at least three alternatives and the social choice rule satisfies
>   **choice from all subsets**
>   **unrestricted preferences**
>   **pairwise independence**
>   **weak Pareto**
and if social choices satisfy rationality conditions RC1 and RC3

Note a matter of importance for chapter 6. In the proof of this theorem, we use the preferences of table 3.4 which involves at least three varieties of individual preferences (the set entitled 'rest' may be empty, but none of the other sets in that table can be empty). Furthermore, the first three varieties of preferences in that table are those that can give a voting cycle with majority voting.

Note also, however, that theorem 3.6 is unnecessary if there are only two people. Then there cannot be two fully decisive sets with only some members in common, and so D^* consists of both people, or of only one of them.

3.9 Proof of Arrow's theorem: the dictator

If the collective contains two or more members, it is possible to divide society into two parts (E and the rest), each containing some members of the collective. Since neither part contains the whole collective, neither is fully decisive, nor even semidecisive over any two alternatives (else it would be fully decisive because of the epidemic). So, with preferences consistent with the restrictions of table 3.5, $C(a,b) = \{a,b\}$ (if only one of a and b were chosen then one or other set would be semidecisive). Similarly $C(a,c) = \{a,c\}$. Then RC2 implies that $C(b,c) = \{b,c\}$, which contradicts weak Pareto because everyone prefers c to b.

Table 3.5 Preferences demonstrating dictatorship

individuals	preferences consistent with
in E	aP_icP_ib
rest	cP_ibP_ia

This contradiction arises because we have divided society into two parts, each containing some members of the collective. It can be avoided only if it is impossible to make this division; that is, if the collective has only one member. Such an individual is a dictator. So we have proved:

Theorem 3.7 There is a dictator if there are at least three alternatives and the social choice rule satisfies
> **choice from all subsets**
> **unrestricted preferences**
> **pairwise independence**
> **weak Pareto**
and if social choices satisfy rationality conditions RC1, RC2 and RC3

Theorem 3.3 is identical to theorem 3.7 except that theorem 3.3 requires full rationality of social choices: that is RC4 also. We have not used RC4 during the proof, so its addition is irrelevant to the proof. Plainly, including RC4 does not remove the inevitability of the dictatorship.

Note that the theorem has been proved for any finite number of people (it is trivial if there is only one person; our proofs hold when there are two or more).

3.10 Alternative versions

Theorem 3.7 can be revised in a variety of ways: the following is justified by theorems 3.1 and 3.2:

Theorem 3.8 There is a dictator if there are at least three alternatives and the social choice rule satisfies
> **choice from all subsets**
> **unrestricted preferences**
> **independence**
> **unanimity**
and if social choices satisfy rationality conditions RC1, RC2 and RC3

Arrow's original version of the theorem is also somewhat different: he does not use the weak Pareto condition, but derives it from two others. These are:

> **non − imposition:** for any two alternatives a and b, there are preferences for which $C(a,b) = \{a\}$ and other preferences for which $C(a,b) = \{b\}$
> **positive responsiveness** (also known as **positive association**): if preferences change from (R_i) to (R'_i) so that aP'_ib whenever aP_ib and aR'_ib whenever aI_ib, then if $C(a,b) = \{a\}$ with preferences (R_i), then $C'(a,b) = \{a\}$ with preferences (R'_i)

The non-imposition condition ensures that there are some circumstances in which each alternative is chosen from a pair. Positive responsiveness considers the effects if some people change from preferring b to a either to indifference or to preferring a to b, or if some change from indifference between a and b to preferring a to b. The position of a relative to b is strengthened – and the condition requires that, if a was previously the sole choice from $\{a,b\}$, then a continues to be the sole choice from $\{a,b\}$. It is very simple to show that these two conditions imply weak Pareto. Start with the preferences (guaranteed to exist by non-imposition) for which a is the sole choice from $\{a,b\}$ and then move to a situation in which everyone prefers a to b, thus strengthening the position of a relative to b as in the condition of positive responsiveness. Then a must be the sole choice from $\{a,b\}$ when everyone prefers a to b – noting that pairwise independence implies that only preferences between a and b can affect the social choice from $\{a,b\}$.

Arrow also does not refer explicitly to rationality conditions such as RC1 to RC4. Instead, he requires that the aggregation procedure should produce complete and transitive social preferences, from which choices could be derived using the Condorcet criterion. Arrows's own version of the theorem is:

Theorem 3.9 There is a dictator if there are at least three alternatives and if the social choice rule gives choices derivable from a complete and transitive social preference relation using the Condorcet criterion and satisfies
>   **unrestricted preferences**
>   **pairwise independence**
>   **non-imposition**
>   **positive responsiveness**

Despite this variation between Arrow's version of the theorem and our own theorem 3.7, we shall refer to all of the related theorems as 'Arrow's theorem' (some authors use 'Arrow's impossibility theorem' because it is impossible to require all the conditions of theorem 3.7 together with the requirement that there should not be a dictator). Many alternative versions and proofs of Arrow's theorem have been put forward: Vickrey (1960), Blau (1957) and others commented on Arrow's original formulation, which Arrow himself discussed in the 1963 revision of his 1951 book. Sen (1970a) provides another standard proof. MacKay (1980) provides a non-technical introduction to Arrow's theorem: his book is subtitled 'A case study in the Philosophy of Economics' – where one might quarrel only with the last word, since MacKay recognises the applicability of the theory beyond economics.

3.11 Strong Pareto and a hierarchy of dictators

The versions of Arrow's theorem that we have so far discussed show that there is an inevitable dictator. The only scope for ambiguity in the social choice arises when the dictator has a choice set containing more than one alternative because he is indifferent between them. The social choice set need not include all of the dictator's most preferred alternatives – though it cannot include any other alternative. Suppose for simplicity that individual 1 is the dictator, and we are interested in the social choice from $\{a,b\}$ when aI_1b. Pairwise independence implies that this social choice is the same as the social choice from $\{a,b\}$ when the dictator is indifferent between all alternatives. We can define a set of individuals D (which does not include 1) to be **semidecisive for a over b when 1 is indifferent** if $C(a,b)$

$= \{a\}$ when everyone in D prefers a to b, 1 is indifferent between a and b and everyone else prefers b to a. Then we can follow all the stages of our proof through as long as:

(i)   we replace weak Pareto by strong Pareto (to cater for the dictator's indifference) and

(ii)   we include 1's indifference between all alternatives as an additional line in every table.

We are essentially examining the choices of society ignoring individual 1 because he is indifferent. We can then demonstrate that there is some other individual (call him 2) whose preference determines the social choice when 1 is indifferent and 2 is not indifferent. We can then repeat the process to consider the social choice when 1 and 2 are indifferent, when another individual can determine the choice – and determine a **hierarchy of dictators**, each of whom has the power to determine the social choice from any pair of alternatives when those 'higher' in the hierarchy are all indifferent between the pair.

So we have:

Theorem 3.10 There is a hierarchy of dictators if there are at least three alternatives and the social choice rule satisfies
    choice from all subsets
    unrestricted preferences
    pairwise independence
    strong Pareto
and if social choices satisfy rationality conditions RC1, RC2 and RC3

3.12 Fixed preferences

Samuelson (see, for example, 1977) and others have disputed that Arrow's theorem prevents us from finding what is known as a **Bergson social welfare function**. It is argued that, in the traditions of welfare economics, it is not necessary for the social choice rule to work for all possible preferences. A Bergson social welfare function needs to be specified only for those preferences that happen to exist. In these circumstances, of course, majority voting (for example) might work because the preferences do not give rise to a voting cycle.

The Samuelson argument looks like an attractive escape route, but Arrow's theorem still points to potential problems (see, for example, Kemp and Ng 1976, Parks 1976) in the specification of a non-dictatorial

Bergson social welfare function. The difficulties arise if there are many alternatives (and hence many potential sets of three alternatives), and if the same method of determining social choices is to be used for each pair of alternatives. For example, if majority voting is used, there is a considerable likelihood that a voting cycle will arise in at least one set of three alternatives.

The condition that the same method of determining social choices is to be used for each pair of alternatives is known as **symmetry**. Stated more formally, symmetry requires that, if a is socially preferred to b when preferences satisfy the restrictions of column I in table 3.6, then c is socially preferred to d when preferences satisfy the restrictions of column II. If the rule satisfies independence as well, then no other information is needed to determine the social preference between a and b or between c and d. The combination of symmetry and independence is known as **neutrality**.

Table 3.6 Preferences illustrating symmetry

| | preferences consistent with | |
individuals	I	II
E	aP_ib	cP_id
F	bP_ia	dP_ic
rest	aI_ib	cI_id

If the social choice rule satisfies symmetry, and there are many alternatives, it is likely that all the patterns of preferences needed in the proof of theorem 3.7 will arise, and so it is possible to show that there is a dictator. Of course, there may not be a dictator (in the extreme, everyone may have the same preferences), but the argument that we have made here demonstrates that the possibility of dictatorship is not completely removed.

3.13 Possible resolutions

We have several versions of Arrow's theorem and much of the rest of this book (and most of the immense literature following from the issues raised in Arrow's book) contains attempts to avoid the apparently inevitable dictatorship. In chapter 4, we consider the possibilities of relaxing the rationality requirements. In chapter 5, we consider removing the independence condition, and in sections 5.5 and 6.5 we relax the requirement that the rule should give a social choice from all subsets of the alternatives. In chapter 6 we examine the possibility of relaxing the requirement that the social choice rule must give a choice for every set of preferences – and, in particular, we identify the range of preferences for which majority voting does not give a voting cycle. These three chapters leave out the possibility of relaxing the unanimity or weak Pareto conditions – and beg the question of whether we might be able to reconcile ourselves to the inevitable dictatorship.

As we said when we introduced the conditions, it is very hard to argue against the unanimity condition, except conceivably in certain ethical contexts where judgements are based on some overriding moral principle to which individuals' preferences are irrelevant. When pairwise independence holds too, unanimity breeds weak Pareto which has been the subject of some critical discussion in the context of judgements involving individual rights. Examples have been put forward in which we might want to abandon the Pareto principle in certain circumstances (and also abandon pairwise independence, else we should have to abandon unanimity, which we may be less inclined to do). We shall look at this in chapter 7.

So, should we care about dictatorship? Certainly in the context of elections, committees and public choices, it is not democratic in any sense to allow one person's view to determine the social choice as a dictator. But what of moral judgements? Many moral standpoints emphasise the duty to take account of other people's interests – in the extreme to 'do to them as you want them to do to you'. Arrow's theorem tells us that there are circumstances in which such altruism is impossible, and this impossibility might be regarded as a justification for morality based on self-interest. The person forming the moral view is the dictator in that his own interests prevail. Most people would probably regard this as a depressing and undesirable conclusion, but much of welfare economics, including Adam Smith's invisible hand, is built on the assumption that individuals are self-interested above all other things. The standard conclusion of welfare economics is that, if everyone is self-interested, the outcome of a competitive economy will be efficient: resources are used in such a way that it is impossible to produce more of one good without diverting resources from producing some other good. In such a system, there is no involuntary unemployment, and no idle capital equipment – and there is no guarantee that people will not be horribly poor. Supporters of such a system might gain comfort from the conclusion of Arrow's theorem that it is not possible for people to be consistently altruistic (except in the trivial sense that one individual might make some other individual's interests paramount – at the expense of his own), but that is cold comfort for those who believe that the best security against starvation is that other people care.

4

Collective rationality

The original version of Arrow's theorem insists that social choices should look as though they were made by a fully rational individual. Such rational social choices are consistent with complete and transitive social preferences, using the Condorcet criterion to determine one from the other. We can only avoid the dictatorship of the previous chapter if we remove at least one of the conditions needed to demonstrate it. In this chapter, we consider the possibility of reducing the rationality conditions. Can we give intuitive meaning to, or examples of, social choice rules that satisfy only some of the conditions RC1 to RC4 for the **collective rationality** of social choices?

To some extent, we start at a disadvantage. The proof of theorem 3.7 does not use RC4, and so the dictator is inevitable even without full collective rationality. The proof of the epidemic and that there is a collective require RC1 and RC3; the inevitable dictator follows when we add RC2.

4.1 Limited path independence

One form of less-than-full collective rationality is **limited path independence**. This is illustrated by using a social choice rule in two ways:

(i)   **directly** to find the choice set $C(T)$ from set T of alternatives,

(ii)   **indirectly** to eliminate alternatives by successive social choices from pairs of alternatives from T. Wherever only one alternative is chosen from a pair, the other alternative is eliminated from further consideration. Continue to make choices from pairs to eliminate as many alternatives as possible. The remaining, non-eliminated alternatives have been chosen by the indirect method. In principle, the outcome of the indirect method depends on the initial and subsequent pairings of alternatives.

The social choice rule satisfies limited path independence if for every set T of the alternatives the indirect method finds the same set of non-eliminated alternatives however the alternatives in T are divided into pairs **and** if this set of alternatives contains $C(T)$. Note that the indirect method may end up finding more alternatives than the direct method – the rule satisfies limited path independence as long as the indirect method eliminates none of the alternatives in $C(T)$.

Consider an athletic analogy. The direct method involves a one kilometre race between all the competitors; all those who finish within five seconds of the winner of the race are chosen to train for the national Olympic squad. In the indirect method, an individual is eliminated from the qualifying rounds of the national one kilometre championships if some other competitor beats him by five seconds or more in a two person race. The system satisfies limited path independence if the candidates who are not eliminated are the same whatever pairings are used in the qualifying rounds and if they include all those who would be selected in the single race.

Pareto extension rules and the first preference rule

One well-established rule that satisfies limited path independence, but does not give fully rational choices is the **weak Pareto extension rule**. This rule chooses from T all alternatives except those to which some other alternative in T is unanimously preferred. In the indirect method, one of a pair of alternatives is eliminated if everyone prefers the other alternative to it. Plainly, in the indirect method, an alternative is eliminated if some other is unanimously preferred to it, as it is in the direct method. So, the rule satisfies limited path independence.

When preferences are very diverse, the choice set from T is likely to be nearly as large as T itself – few alternatives are ruled out by unanimous preference. The choice set can be restricted a little more in some circumstances by using the **strong Pareto extension rule** (we shall refer to either as the **Pareto extension rule**) – this excludes from $C(T)$ an alternative a if there is some other alternative b in T which some prefer to a, and if there is no-one who prefers a to b. The strong Pareto extension rule also satisfies limited path independence.

Pareto extension rules are not particularly discriminating, because they deliberately avoid resolving any conflicts of preference: alternatives are ruled out only by unanimous opinions, or at least opinions that no-one opposes. The **first preference rule** is somewhat more discriminating: the choice set consists of every individual's most preferred alternative(s) from a set. In the indirect method, an alternative is eliminated from a pair if the alternative is no-one's first preference from that pair; that is, if everyone prefers the other alternative. This rule satisfies limited path independence, but note that the indirect method finds a larger set of non-eliminated alternatives than $C(T)$. For example, if preferences are as in table 4.1, the direct method gives $C(a,b,c,d) = \{a,b\}$. However, only d is eliminated in pairwise comparisons, since there is no unanimous preference other than for a over d. The indirect method eliminates only d.

Table 4.1 First preference rule and limited path independence

individual	preferences
1	$aP_1bP_1cP_1d$
2	$bP_2cP_2aP_2d$
3	$aP_3dP_3cP_3b$

Limited path independence and rationality

If a rule gives choices that satisfy limited path independence then the choices satisfy RC1 and RC3. The opposite is also true and so choices satisfy limited path independence if and only if they satisfy both RC1 and RC3. So, from theorems in chapter 3, limited path independence in combination with the other conditions is sufficient to give both the epidemic and the collective.

To see the equivalence of limited path independence and the pair of rationality conditions RC1 and RC3, suppose first that choices satisfy RC1 and RC3:

(i)   **To show that the indirect method always eliminates the same alternatives.** Suppose that the indirect method is used twice. On occasion I, c is eliminated; on occasion II, c is not eliminated. There is therefore some set of alternatives X consisting of all those that can eliminate c: $X = \{x \mid C(x,c) = x\}$. On occasion I, some alternative in X eliminates c. On occasion II, all alternatives in X must be eliminated before any is used 'against' *c*. Suppose that, in II, *b* is the last alternative in *X* to be eliminated; then $C(a,b) = \{a\}$ for some alternative *a* which is not in *X*. So we have $C(b,c) = \{b\}$ (since *b* is in *X*), $C(a,b) = \{a\}$ (because *a* eliminates *b*) and *c* is in $C(a,c)$ because *a* is not in *X*. These choices contradict RC1. So, if RC1 holds, the indirect method always eliminates the same alternatives.

(ii)   **To show that the indirect method does not eliminate any alternative in $C(T)$.** If *a* is in $C(T)$, RC3 implies that *a* is in $C(a,b)$ for any *b* in *T*, and so *a* is never eliminated in a pairwise choice with any other alternative in *T*.

These two arguments show that, if RC1 and RC3 both hold, then so does limited path independence. Now consider the converse – suppose that choices satisfy limited path independence:

(iii)   **To show that RC1 holds.** Suppose that RC1 does not hold: $C(a,b) = \{a\}$, $C(b,c) = \{b\}$ but *c* is in $C(a,c)$. If we use the indirect method, taking $\{a,b\}$ as the first pair eliminates *b*, leaving $\{a,c\}$ so that *c* cannot be eliminated. Alternatively, taking $\{b,c\}$ as the first pair eliminates *c*. The two uses of the indirect method do not lead to the same set of non-eliminated alternatives. So, if RC1 does not hold, limited path independence does not hold. Put the other way around, if limited path independence holds, so does RC1.

(iv)   **To show that RC3 holds.** If *a* is in $C(T)$, the indirect method cannot eliminate *a* in any pairing. So *a* is in $C(a,b)$ for any other *b* in *T* and RC3 holds.

Together, these four arguments prove:

Theorem 4.1 The choice sets given by a choice rule satisfy RC1 and RC3 if and only if they satisfy limited path independence

Theorem 4.1, along with the proof of the existence of a collective in section 3.6, implies:

Theorem 4.2 There is a collective if there are at least three alternatives and if a social choice rule satisfies
>   **choice from all subsets**
>   **unrestricted preferences**
>   **pairwise independence**
>   **weak Pareto**
and gives choice sets that satisfy limited path independence

4.2 Path independence

Limited path independence introduces the idea that we might find the choice set from T in an indirect way. **Path independence** (first introduced by Plott, 1973) takes this idea further: we divide a set V of alternatives into two parts, T and U, which together contain all the alternatives in V (T and U may contain some common alternatives). $C(V)$ is determined by the social choice rule as are $C(T)$ and $C(U)$. If we take the chosen alternatives from T and from U (that is, $C(T) \cup C(U)$), we can find the choice set from these alternatives (that is, $C[C(T) \cup C(U)]$). If this choice set is the same as $C(V)$, then the social choices are path independent.

Formally, choices are path independent if, for any set V of alternatives divided into T and U (so that $T \cup U = V$), $C(V) = C[C(T) \cup C(U)]$. The notation may seem confusing: $C[C(T) \cup C(U)]$ is the choice from the combination of two sets $C(T)$ and $C(U)$ which are themselves choice sets.

The Pareto extension rules and the first preference rule give path independent choices. If a rule gives path independent social choices, it plainly gives choices that satisfy limited path independence, and so theorem 4.2 implies:

Theorem 4.3 There is a collective if there are at least three alternatives, if the social choice rule gives path independent social choices and satisfies
>   **choice from all subsets**
>   **unrestricted preferences**
>   **weak Pareto**
>   **pairwise independence**

However, there are rules that give choices satisfying limited path independence, that satisfy unrestricted preferences, weak Pareto and pairwise independence (and so give a collective) but which do not give path independent choices. For example, consider the rule defined by the following two statements:

(i)   If T contains four or more alternatives, $C(T)$ is determined as in the weak Pareto extension rule.

(ii)   If T contains two or three alternatives, $C(T)$ is determined as in the first preference rule.

This rule satisfies RC1: if $C(a,b) = \{a\}$ and $C(b,c) = \{b\}$ then a is everyone's first preference from $\{a,b\}$ and b is everyone's first preference from $\{b,c\}$, and so everyone prefers a to c, so that $C(a,c) = \{a\}$. It satisfies RC3 also: if a is chosen from T which has three members including b, then a is chosen from $\{a,b\}$ because the first preference rule satisfies RC3; if a is chosen from T which has four or more members including b, then not everyone prefers b to a, so that a is chosen from $\{a,b\}$. However, this hybrid rule does not give path independent choices as the preferences of table 4.2 demonstrate. The rule gives the choice sets of table 4.3.

Table 4.2 Preferences for hybrid social choice rule

individual	preferences
1	$aP_1cP_1dP_1b$
2	$bP_2dP_2aP_2c$
3	$aP_3bP_3cP_3d$

We test path independence by dividing $\{a,b,c,d\}$ into $\{a,c\}$ and $\{a,b,d\}$:

(i) $C(a,b,c,d) = \{a,b,d\}$,

(ii) $C(a,c) = \{a\}$, $C(a,b,d) = \{a,b\}$; $C(a,c) \cup C(a,b,d) = \{a,b\}$, and $C[C(a,c) \cup C(a,b,d)] = C(a,b) = \{a,b\}$.

So $C[C(a,c) \cup C(a,b,d)] \neq C(a,b,c,d)$ and choices are not path independent.

If choices satisfy path independence (or limited path independence) and the other conditions hold, there is a collective. Some set of individuals – perhaps the whole society – can impose its will when it has a unanimous preference. The inevitability of a collective, particularly if it contains a large fraction of society, is perhaps more welcome than the inevitability of a dictator which Arrow's theorem implies. However, it remains true that a set of individuals that has the ability to decide one issue has the ability to decide any issue – the epidemic proposition holds. As we discussed in chapter 3, this is not likely to pose a problem for electoral systems and in some other public policy choices, but certainly in the realm of ethical

Table 4.3 Choice sets with preferences of table 4.2, using hybrid social
choice rule

set	choice set
{a,b,c,d}	{a,b,d}
{a,b,c}	{a,b}
{a,b,d}	{a,b}
{a,c,d}	{a,d}
{b,c,d}	{b,c}
{a,b}	{a,b}
{a,c}	{a}
{a,d}	{a,d}
{b,c}	{b,c}
{b,d}	{b,d}
{c,d}	{c,d}

judgements, this epidemic disallows many issue-specific judgements based
for example on individual rights. So, although we escape the dictatorship
by not insisting on full rationality, many problems remain unresolved.
Indeed, it would be fair to say that neither the Pareto extension rule nor
the first preference rule (nor the hybrid of table 4.2) resolves serious
differences of opinion. The Pareto extension rule only excludes an
alternative if there is some other alternative that everyone would accept in
its place. The first preference rule does not exclude any alternative that
someone holds as her first preference. So these rules essentially make easy
choices, but do not resolve difficult ones. They may be useful for
narrowing down the set of alternatives, but they are not likely to lead to
the choice of a single alternative.

4.3 Quasitransitivity and oligarchy

Our consideration of path independent choice rules does not enquire
about the possibility that the social choices are derivable from social
preferences using the Condorcet criterion – allowing that social preferences need not be transitive. If we are to use the Condorcet criterion,
choices must satisfy RC3 and RC4 (see section 2.3). If they also satisfy
limited path independence, they must satisfy RC1 as well.

If a social choice rule gives social preferences (for which we use the
notation R, P and I without subscripts) that satisfy RC1, the preferences

must satisfy *PP* transitivity (see section 2.2). A preference relation that is *PP* transitive but not necessarily *II* transitive (for which RC2 would be needed as well) is **quasitransitive.** Quasitransitivity was introduced by Sen (1969).

Choices given by the Pareto extension rule (weak or strong version) can be derived from quasitransitive social preferences using the Condorcet criterion. For the strong Pareto extension rule, *aPb* if some individual(s) prefer *a* to *b* and no-one prefers *b* to *a*. Then *aPb* and *bPc* imply *aPc* as some individual must prefer *a* to *c* and no-one prefers *c* to *a*. However, statements involving social indifference may not be transitive (because RC2 need not hold), as the preferences of table 4.4 show. With those individual preferences, the social preferences given by the Pareto extension rule are *bPc*, *aIc*, *aIb*, which are not *II* transitive.

Quasitransitivity of social preferences and the use of the Condorcet criterion involves RC4, and so is not the same as path independence. The first preference rule gives path independent social choices, but the choices do not necessarily satisfy RC4 as we see in table 4.5 where $C(b,c) = \{b,c\}$ and $C(a,c) = \{a,c\}$ but *c* is not in $C(a,b,c)$. Thus the first preference rule gives path independent choices but these cannot be derived from quasitransitive social preferences using the Condorcet criterion.

Table 4.4 Preferences showing failure of RC2 with Pareto rule

individual	preferences
1	bP_1cP_1a
2	aP_2bP_2c

Table 4.5 Preferences showing failure of RC4 with first preference rule

individual	preference
1	aP_1cP_1b
2	bP_2cP_2a

When a rule gives path independent choices, theorem 4.1 tells us that there is a collective which can, by unanimous view, exclude an alternative from the choice set. If the choices can be derived from a quasitransitive social preference relation using the Condorcet criterion, then each

Table 4.6 Preferences demonstrating oligarchy

	preferences consistent with	
individuals	I	II
in E	cP_ia	$cP'_iaP'_ib$
in F	aI_ic	$aI'_icP'_ib$
rest (including j)	aP_ic	$aP'_ibP'_ic$

member of the collective has an additional power: whatever preferences others have, she can ensure that her own first preference in a set of alternatives is amongst those chosen. A set of individuals who form a collective with the additional power that each member can ensure that her own first preference is chosen from any set is known as an **oligarchy**. The first results relating to oligarchies can be found in Gibbard (1969), in Guha (1972) and in Mas-Colell and Sonnenschein (1972).

To see this, suppose that that the choice rule satisfies all the conditions of Arrow's theorem except that social choices can be derived from quasitransitive but not transitive social preferences, so that RC1, RC3 and RC4 hold. There is a collective (for which RC1 and RC3 are needed), but not necessarily a dictator (for which we used RC2). Individual j in the collective prefers a to all other alternatives in T. Suppose that a is not chosen from T. If RC4 holds, there is some other alternative c in T for which $C(a,c) = \{c\}$ (if this were not so, we could combine all pairs $\{a,b\}$, $\{a,c\}$, etc. in T and build up the choice set from T ensuring that it contains a). In the preferences of column I in table 4.6, E is the set of those who prefer c to a and F is the set of those who are indifferent between a and c. Individual j is in neither E nor F. Then consider preferences consistent with column II in table 4.6. By pairwise independence, $C'(a,c) = \{c\}$ because $C(a,c) = \{c\}$; weak Pareto gives $C'(a,b) = \{a\}$, and so RC1 gives $C'(b,c) = \{c\}$. Thus the members of E and F together form a set that is semidecisive for c over b. By theorem 3.5, $E \cup F$ is fully decisive, and should therefore contain all the members of the collective, including j. However, by construction, it does not contain j, and we have a contradiction based on the presumption that a is not in $C(T)$. Therefore a must be in $C(T)$ if it is j's first preference and we have proved:

Theorem 4.4 There is an oligarchy if there are at least three alternatives, if the social choice rule satisfies

    choice from all subsets

    unrestricted preferences

    pairwise independence

    weak Pareto

and if social choices can be derived from quasitransitive social preferences using the Condorcet criterion (so that RC1, RC3 and RC4 hold).

Examples of such a social choice rule are the Pareto extension rules.

The simplest example of a rule that gives path independent choices that cannot be derived from quasitransitive social preferences using the Condorcet criterion is the first preference rule – but this rule also gives an oligarchy trivially. Every individual's first preference is, by definition, chosen. So RC4 is not necessary for an oligarchy. However, if RC1 and RC3 hold but RC4 does not, there can be a collective but not an oligarchy, as the following rule illustrates when there are three alternatives:

(i) $C(a,b) = \{a\}$ if everyone prefers a to b; $C(a,b) = \{b\}$ if everyone prefers b to a; otherwise $C(a,b) = \{a,b\}$.

(ii) $h(a)$ is the number of individuals for whom neither b nor c is preferred to a; similarly for $h(b)$ and $h(c)$.

(iii) $C(a,b,c) = \{a\}$ if $h(b) = h(c) = 0$, and similarly for b and c.

(iv) $C(a,b,c) = \{a,b\}$ if $h(a) > h(c)$ and $h(b) > h(c)$ – with similar rules for other pairs.

(v)   otherwise $C(a,b,c) = \{a,b,c\}$.

So, in choosing from $\{a,b,c\}$, we take the uniquely most preferred alternative if there is one. If there is no uniquely most preferred alternative, then we take the two alternatives that are more individuals' first preference than the third if this gives a clear cut decision (i.e. if there is a clear 'loser' in this sense). Otherwise we choose all three. RC1 holds: $C(a,b) = \{a\}$ implies that everyone prefers a to b; $C(b,c) = \{b\}$ implies that everyone prefers b to c; if both hold, then everyone prefers a to c, so that $C(a,c) = \{a\}$. RC3 also holds: if a is chosen from $\{a,b,c\}$ then $h(a) > 0$ and so it is not true that everyone prefers b to a or that everyone prefers c to a; so a is chosen from $\{a,b\}$ and $\{a,c\}$. However, the choice from $\{a,b,c\}$ cannot always be derived from choices from the three pairs using the Condorcet criterion as the preferences of table 4.7 show. With these preferences $C(a,c) = \{a,c\}$, $C(b,c) = \{b,c\}$, and so RC4 implies that c would be chosen from $\{a,b,c\}$. However, $h(a) = 2$, $h(b) = 2$ and $h(c) =$

Table 4.7 Preferences showing that a collective need not be an oligarchy

individual	preferences
1,2	aP_ibP_ic
3,4	bP_icP_ia
5	cP_5bP_5a

1 and so c is not chosen from $\{a,b,c\}$. RC4 does not necessarily hold, and the choice from $\{a,b,c\}$ cannot always be derived using the Condorcet criterion. With this rule, the collective is the whole society, but individual 5 is not able to ensure that c is chosen from $\{a,b,c\}$, and so the collective is not an oligarchy. This example illustrates that there may be a collective that is not an oligarchy.

4.4 Acyclic preferences and extended majority voting

If a social choice rule gives choices that can be derived from a social preference relation using the Condorcet criterion and gives a choice from all subsets of the alternatives, the social preferences cannot include cycles. A cycle such as aPb, bPc, cPd and dPa would imply that $C(a,b,c,d)$ is empty. Thus the underlying social preference relation from which the choice sets can be derived must be **acyclic**.

Choices can be derived from a social preference relation using the Condorcet criterion if and only if the choices satisfy RC3 and RC4. RC3 and RC4 are not sufficient to give a collective, or even to demonstrate the epidemic theorem. Consider the social choice rule (for three alternatives and many people) defined as follows:

(i) $n(aP_ib)$ is the number of individuals who prefer a to b, and similarly for other preferences.

(ii) $C(a,b) = $ $\{a\}$ if $n(aP_ib) > 3n(bP_ia)$,
  $\{b\}$ if $n(bP_ia) > 3n(aP_ib)$,
  $\{a,b\}$ otherwise.

(iii) $C(a,c) = $ $\{a\}$ if $n(aP_ic) > 3n(cP_ia)$,
  $\{c\}$ if $n(cP_ia) > 3n(aP_ic)$,
  $\{a,c\}$ otherwise.

(iv) $C(b,c) = $ $\{b\}$ if $n(bP_ic) > n(cP_ib)$,
  $\{c\}$ if $n(cP_ib) > n(bP_ic)$,
  $\{b,c\}$ if $n(bP_ic) = n(cP_ib)$.

(v)   These choices from pairs are used to define a social preference relation using the Condorcet criterion. We then use that relation and the Condorcet criterion to define $C(a,b,c)$.

The cycle aPb, bPc, cPa is impossible, because (ignoring individual indifference) aPb requires that <u>more</u> <u>than</u> three quarters prefer a to b, bPc requires that <u>more</u> <u>than</u> half prefer b to c, so more than one quarter must prefer a to b and b to c – so that more than one quarter prefer a to c, and hence aRc.

This is an example of a general version of **extended majority voting**: in Craven (1971), (1988), I demonstrate the majorities that are necessary to avoid a cycle of social preferences, and the more convoluted argument that shows that individual indifference does not affect the conclusion. In brief the conclusion is as follows. The **required fraction** for a over b is the minimum proportion of those who are not indifferent between a and b needed to give $C(a,b) = \{a\}$. For example, the required fraction is 3/4 if the rule gives $C(a,b) = \{a\}$ if $n(aP_ib) \geqslant 3n(bP_ia)$. If the rule gives $C(a,b) = \{a\}$ only when $n(aP_ib) > 3n(bP_ia)$, the required fraction is the smallest fraction over 3/4 that is possible with the given population (some of whom might be indifferent). For example, with 12 people, the smallest possible fraction above 3/4 is 7/9 ($= 0.777...$).

A cycle of three alternatives (such as aPb, bPc, cPa) is impossible if and only if the sum of the required fractions for a over b, b over c and c over a exceeds two. A cycle of four alternatives cannot occur if and only if the sum of the four required fractions exceeds three. A cycle of m alternatives cannot occur if and only if the sum of the m required fractions exceeds $m - 1$. In our example, the sum on any cycle of three alternatives exceeds $3/4 + 3/4 + 1/2 = 2$, which is sufficient to avoid a cycle. Simple majority voting (a required fraction of just over one half in each case) gives a sum of required fractions just exceeding 1.5, which is insufficient, as the voting paradox illustrates.

In the example, the rule uses a simple majority to choose a single alternative from $C(b,c)$; but a majority of more than 3:1 is needed to choose a single alternative from either of the other pairs. However, RC1 need not hold: for example if, in 100 people, 49 hold cP_iaP_ib, 27 hold aP_ibP_ic and 24 hold bP_icP_ia, then $C(a,b) = \{a\}$, $C(b,c) = \{b\}$, but $C(a,c) = \{a,c\}$ (the majority for c over a is $73 - 27$ – insufficient to give cPa). We use RC1 to demonstrate the epidemic, and in this case there is no epidemic – any set of 51 per cent of the individuals is semidecisive for c

over b, but no such set is semidecisive for a over c. There can be no collective because any set of more than three-quarters of the individuals can ensure the exclusion of any of the alternatives, but no smaller set can do this – so that there is no unique smallest fully decisive set that is a collective.

We have seen in this chapter that reducing the rationality requirement avoids the inevitable dictator – and depending on the conditions that we require, we may have a collective, an oligarchy or neither. However, the cost of this 'rescue' from the dictatorship of Arrow's theorem is that the choice process is indecisive in many cases. Pareto extension rules resolve no conflicts of preferences; if someone prefers a to b and someone prefers b to a, then neither a nor b is excluded from $C(a,b)$. The first preference rule goes a little further, but still leaves many important conflicts unresolved, and the rule that requires large majorities (such as 3:1 or 4:1) also fails to exclude any alternative that has at least some measure of support. None of these rules resolves as many conflicts of preferences as does simple majority voting, which would resolve most conflicts if only it did not give the voting paradox.

Appendix: Conventional rationality conditions

The four rationality conditions RC1 to RC4 occurred 'naturally' in our discussion: there is an alternative collection of rationality conditions in the literature which can be used instead. Sen (1977a) gives an extensive survey of various rationality conditions the first of which were introduced in Sen (1969) and discussed in Sen (1970). These conditions have advantages in certain circumstances, and in some cases they also have revealing interpretations. The conditions have, thanks to Sen, names from the Greek alphabet which we preserve:

Condition α: **if** (i) alternative a is chosen from T **and** (ii) a is in U which is a subset of T, **then** a is chosen from U

Condition α would be the same as our RC3 if U were a set of two alternatives. In condition α, U can be a subset of any size within T.

Condition ε: **if** (i) U is a subset of T **and** (ii) U contains $C(T)$ **then** $C(T)$ is not a proper subset of $C(U)$

(Note that the only subsets of X that are not proper subsets of X are the empty set and X itself: a convoluted statement that demonstrates an advantage of common sense over rigour).

Intuitively, condition ε requires that, if U is a subset of T (and hence smaller than T), the choice set from U cannot be larger than (that is, contain) the choice set from T.

Condition γ: **if** a is chosen from T and from U **then** a is chosen from $T \cup U$

Condition γ would be the same as RC4 if U was a pair of alternatives including a. Condition γ considers the combination of any two sets.

Condition ß: **if** (i) a and b are both chosen from U **and** (ii) U is a subset of T **and** (iii) if a is chosen from T **then** b is chosen from T.

Intuitively, condition ß requires equal treatment: if a and b are both chosen from U, then neither or both (that is, not just one) of them is chosen from any set T which contains U.

There is a variety of results involving these Greek-named conditions and our own RC1 to RC4:

Theorem 4.5

(i)   If α holds then ß holds if and only if ε, γ and RC2 all hold.

(ii)   Conditions α, ε, γ and RC2 are independent (that is, any three of them can hold true even if the fourth does not).

(iii)   α and ε together imply RC1.

(iv)   α implies RC3.

(v)   γ implies RC4.

(vi)   RC3 and RC4 together imply α and γ.

(vii)   RC1, RC3 and RC4 together imply ε.

(viii)   RC1 to RC4 together imply ß.

(ix)   Choices are path independent if and only if both α and ε hold.

(x)   Choices can be derived from a preference relation using the Condorcet criterion if and only if both α and γ hold (such choices are known as binary or normal in various parts of the literature).

(xi)   Choices can be derived from a quasitransitive preference relation using the Condorcet criterion if and only if all of α, γ and ε hold.

(xii)   Choices can be derived from a transitive preference relation using the Condorcet criterion if and only if both α and ß hold.

These propositions are reported here mainly to relate our own rationality conditions and their consequences to those used in other places. In other parts of the literature, our own RC3 has been called α2.

Translated into these Greek-named conditions, our theorems give that, along with Arrow's other conditions, α and ε are sufficient for there to be a collective; α, γ and ε are sufficient for there to be an oligarchy; α and β are sufficient for a dictatorship.

Proof of theorem 4.5

(i)   Suppose α and β hold. Suppose U is a subset of T, $C(T)$ is a subset of $C(U)$, $a \in C(U)$, $a \notin C(T)$ (so that ε does not hold). Take $b \in C(T)$: α implies $b \in C(U)$, which contradicts β. So α & β implies ε. Suppose $a \in C(U) \cap C(V)$, $a \notin C(U \cup V)$ (so that γ does not hold). Take $b \in C(U \cup V)$. Then $b \in C(U) \cup C(V)$. If $b \in C(U)$, then $a \in C(U)$ & $b \in C(U \cup V)$ & $a \notin C(U \cup V)$ contradicts β. So α & β implies γ. Finally β trivially implies RC2. Suppose α, ε, γ and RC2 all hold, a, $b \in C(U)$, U is a subset of T, $a \in C(T)$: α implies $C(a,b) = \{a,b\}$ and $a \in C(a,x)$ for all $x \in T$. Take any $x \in T$, $x \neq a$, b; RC2 implies $C(a,b,x) = \{x\}$ or $\{a,b\}$ or $\{a,b,x\}$. Since $a \in C(a,x)$, α & ε implies $C(a,b,x) \neq \{x\}$. So $b \in C(a,b,x)$ for all $x \in T$. Repeated applications of γ then imply $b \in C(T)$. So α & ε & γ & RC2 implies β.

(ii)   Table 4.8 gives examples in which three conditions hold but not the fourth.

Table 4.8 Independence of conditions α, γ, ε and RC2

	choice sets satisfying			
set	ε γ RC2 not α	α γ RC2 not ε	α ε RC2 not γ	α ε γ not RC2
$\{a,b,c\}$	$\{a,b\}$	$\{a\}$	$\{b,c\}$	$\{a,b\}$
$\{a,b\}$	$\{a,b\}$	$\{a,b\}$	$\{a,b\}$	$\{a,b\}$
$\{a,c\}$	$\{c\}$	$\{a\}$	$\{a,c\}$	$\{a,c\}$
$\{b,c\}$	$\{b\}$	$\{c\}$	$\{b,c\}$	$\{b\}$

(iii)   If $C(a,b) = \{a\}$ and $C(b,c) = \{b\}$ then α implies $C(a,b,c) = \{a\}$, and ε implies $C(a,c) = \{a\}$. So RC1 holds.

(iv)   and (v) Trivial.

(vi)   If $a \in C(T)$, $a \in U$ and U is a subset of T, then RC3 implies $a \in C(a,x)$ for all $x \in U$. Then repeated use of RC4 implies $a \in C(U)$, so α holds. If $a \in C(U) \cap C(V)$ then RC3 implies $a \in C(a,x)$ for all $x \in U \cup V$. Repeated use of RC4 implies $a \in C(U \cup V)$ so γ holds.

(vii) Suppose U is a subset of T, $C(T)$ is a subset of $C(U)$, $a \in C(U)$, $a \notin C(T)$. Then by RC4 there is $b \in T$ such that $C(a,b) = \{b\}$. By RC3, $a \in C(a,x)$ for all $x \in U$ and so $b \notin U$. Since $C(T)$ is a subset of $C(U)$, $b \notin C(T)$. So, by RC4 there is $c \in T$ such that $c \neq a$ and $C(b,c) = \{c\}$. Then, by RC1, $C(a,c) = \{c\}$. So $c \notin U$, and hence $c \notin C(T)$. So, by RC4 there is $d \in T$ such that $d \neq a$, $d \neq c$ and $C(c,d) = \{d\}$. Then, by RC1, $C(a,d) = \{d\}$. So $d \notin U$, and hence $d \notin C(T)$. Repeating this, we exhaust the whole of $T-U$ and end with a contradiction. So no such U, T, a can exist. Hence ε holds.

(viii) Follows from (vi), (vii) and (i).

(ix) Suppose $a \in C(T)$, $a \in U$ and U is a subset of T. If choices are path independent, $C(T) = C[C(T-U) \cup C(U)]$. $a \in U$ implies $a \notin C(T-U)$. Hence $a \in C(T)$ implies $a \in C(U)$, and α holds. Suppose $a \in C(U)$, U is a subset of T and $C(T)$ is a subset of $C(U)$. Then $a \in [C(T) \cup C(U)] = C(U)$. α implies $a \in C[C(U)] = C[C(T) \cup C(U)]$. So by path independence, $a \in C(T)$ since $T = T \cup U$. Hence $C(T) = C(U)$ and ε holds. Conversely, suppose that α and ε hold and that $a \in C(U \cup V)$. Then α implies $a \in [C(U) \cup C(V)]$) which is a subset of $(U \cup V)$. Using α again, $a \in C[C(U) \cup C(V)]$. Hence $C(U \cup V)$ is a subset of $C[C(U) \cup C(V)]$. But $[C(U) \cup C(V)]$ is a subset of $(U \cup V)$, and ε implies $C(U \cup V) = C[C(U) \cup C(V)]$. So path independence holds.

(x) We know that choices can be derived from a preference relation using the Condorcet criterion if and only if RC3 and RC4 hold. The result follows from (iv), (v) and (vi).

(xi) The relation is quasitransitive if and only if RC1 holds. The result follows from (x), (iii) and (vii).

(xii) The relation is transitive if and only if RC1 and RC2 both hold. The result follows from (xi) and (i).

5

Strategic manipulation of choice rules

In section 3.3 we discussed briefly the relation between the independence condition and the possibility that individuals might state a false preference in order to change the outcome of the social choice rule. With independence the scope for this sort of manipulation is very limited and so there is a close relation between independence and any requirement that people should not be able to gain by stating a false preference. Unfortunately, independence plays a major role in demonstrating the inevitability of dictatorship. So it would appear likely that, if we want a social choice rule that gives no-one any opportunity for gaining by stating a false preference and that satisfies others of the conditions of Arrow's theorem, we will end up with a dictator. Even with less stringent rationality requirements than those of Arrow's theorem, we are likely to have an oligarchy or a collective.

There are many social choice rules that satisfy all of Arrow's conditions except independence – including rules that give choices that can be derived from a complete and transitive social preference relation using the Condorcet criterion. For example, the first-past-the-post electoral system, satisfies all of the conditions except independence. Independence fails with first-past-the-post because it is plainly necessary to know preferences concerning all of the alternatives to determine which is most preferred by most people.

5.1 Non-manipulable social choice rules

We need to define non-manipulability formally. Consider two sets of preferences (R_i) and (R'_i), in which R_i is the same as R'_i for every individual except j. Using a social choice rule, the two sets of preferences give choice sets $C(T)$ and $C'(T)$ from set T of alternatives. If, according to his preference R_j, j prefers $C'(T)$ to $C(T)$, then he can obtain a more preferred choice set by stating R'_j when he truly holds R_j. In this case, the social choice rule is **open to manipulation by** j **on** T (note that the rule is also open to manipulation by j on T if, when he truly holds R'_j, he prefers $C(T)$ to $C'(T)$. Then he can gain by stating R_j instead of his true preference R'_j). A rule is **non-manipulable** if it is not open to manipulation by any individual on any set of alternatives.

One question remains: a rule is open to manipulation by j on T if j prefers $C'(T)$ to $C(T)$ when he truly holds R_j, but we have not specified how we might derive his preferences about sets of alternatives (potentially containing more than one alternative) from his preferences about single alternatives. We discussed this problem in chapter 2, where we introduced the maximin criterion, which we shall use later in this chapter. For the first part of the chapter, we shall need only the 'obvious' preferences – for example, that if aP_jb, then:

$$\{a\}P_j\{a,b\}P_j\{b\}$$
$$\{a,c\}P_j\{b,c\}$$
etc.

Non-manipulability has a number of important consequences that are very useful in demonstrating theorems with similar outcomes to Arrow's theorem. Assuming that the rule is non-manipulable, we have the following:

NM1   Assume that j truly prefers a to all other alternatives in T and that everyone's preferences are kept unchanged except those of j. Then if j can ensure that a is the sole choice from T by stating some other preference R'_j, then a must be the sole choice from T when j states his true preference R_j.

Otherwise j can gain by stating R'_j instead of his true preference R_j.

NM2   Assume that j truly prefers all other alternatives in T to a and that everyone's preferences are kept unchanged except those of j. Then if a is the sole choice from T when j states his true preference R_j, then a is the sole choice from T whatever preference j states.

Otherwise j could avoid the social choice of a alone by stating some preference other than R_j.

NM1 and NM2 consider what happens if one individual's preference changes. We can consider also the effects of several changes made in turn when a set of individuals change their preferences. We can consider the change in the choice set as each in turn changes – assuming that those who have already switched from R_i to R'_i retain R'_i. Then assuming that the rule is non-manipulable, we have the following:

NM3   Assume that every individual changes in turn from R_i to R'_i, that no individual's preference between a and b changes so that $R_i \mid \{a,b\} = R'_i \mid \{a,b\}$, and that no-one is indifferent between a and b. Then, throughout the sequence of changes in preference, the choice set from $\{a,b\}$ does not change. Hence $C(a,b) = C'(a,b)$.

To show this, suppose for example that aP_jb (and hence aP'_jb) and that the choice set from $\{a,b\}$ changes from $\{a\}$ to $\{a,b\}$ when j changes from R_j to R'_j. When j's true preference is R'_j he can gain by stating R_j instead and so the rule is manipulable. Similar examples apply if j prefers b to a, and however the choice set from $\{a,b\}$ changes.

5.2 Non-manipulability and the proof of Arrow's theorem

To investigate the effect of replacing independence with non-manipulability, we look at a social choice rule that satisfies choice from all subsets, unrestricted preferences, non-manipulability, weak Pareto, and whose choices satisfy either:

(i)   limited path independence (see section 4.1), so that RC1 and RC3 hold, or

(ii)   consistency with a social preference relation using the Condorcet criterion, so that RC3 and RC4 hold.

How does the change from independence to non-manipulability affect the proof of the inevitability of dictatorship? Remember that, in the absence of independence, the choice from any set can depend on preferences concerning alternatives not in that set, as well as on preferences concerning alternatives in that set.

Semidecisiveness

Set D of individuals is semidecisive for a over b if $C(a,b) = \{a\}$ when everyone in D prefers a to b and everyone else prefers b to a. Consider preferences consistent with column I in table 5.1. Preferences concerning

Table 5.1 Preferences demonstrating the epidemic of semidecisiveness

	preferences consistent with	
individuals	I	II
in D	$aP_ibP_icP_i$rest	$aP'_icP'_i$rest
others	$bP_icP_iaP_i$rest	$cP'_iaP'_i$rest

a, b and c are the same as in column I of table 3.2. If D is semidecisive for a over b, $C(a,b) = \{a\}$, and by weak Pareto $C(b,c) = \{b\}$. RC3 implies that $C(a,b,c) = \{a\}$. When R'_i are the true preferences of all members of D, NM1 implies that the choice from $\{a,b,c\}$ is unchanged when any member of D changes from R_i to R'_i else such an individual could gain by stating R_i when he truly holds R'_i. When R_i are the true preferences of everyone not in D, NM2 implies that the choice from $\{a,b,c\}$ is unchanged when anyone not in D changes from R_i to R'_i. So $C'(a,b,c) = \{a\}$. By weak Pareto, $C'(b,c) = \{c\}$. The form of the argument now depends on whether RC1 or RC4 holds.

(i)   RC1 implies $C(a,c) = \{a\}$, and NM3 implies $C'(a,c) = \{a\}$.
(ii) $C'(b,c) = \{c\}$, and so, if c is in $C'(a,c)$ then RC4 implies c is in $C'(a,b,c)$, which it is not. So $C'(a,c) = \{a\}$.

In either case, $C'(a,c) = \{a\}$ when those in D prefer a to c, and those not in D prefer c to a. NM3 implies that, if $C(a,c) = \{a\}$ for one set of preferences for which everyone in D prefers a to c, and everyone else prefers c to a, then the choice set from $\{a,c\}$ is $\{a\}$ whenever such preferences over $\{a,c\}$ occur. So D is semidecisive for a over c.

In a similar way (using preferences related to those in columns I and II of table 3.2) we can show that, if D is semidecisive for a over b, then D is semidecisive for d over b, and then that D is a semidecisive set.

The epidemic

The full epidemic proposition follows by considering the restrictions on preferences in table 5.2, where a is in T and x is any alternative. If D is semidecisive, $C'(a,x) = \{a\}$ for any preferences consistent with column II. As each individual in D changes in turn from R'_i(column II) to R_i (column I) the choice set from $\{a,x\}$ must remain $\{a\}$, else the individual has an

Table 5.2 Preferences showing the full epidemic

	preferences consistent with	
individuals	I	II
in D	$aP_i\text{rest}$	aP'_ix
others	any preference	xP'_ia

incentive to state R'_i when he truly holds R_i. As each individual not in D changes in turn from R'_i to R_i the choice set from $\{a,x\}$ must remain as $\{a\}$, else the individual has an incentive to state R_i when he truly holds R'_i. So $C(a,x) = \{a\}$ for any x in T, and RC3 implies that $C(T) = \{a\}$. The semidecisive set D is fully decisive and we have shown:

Theorem 5.1 If D is semidecisive for a over b, then D is fully decisive if there are at least three alternatives and the social choice rule satisfies

> **choice from all subsets**
> **unrestricted preferences**
> **weak Pareto**
> **non-manipulability**

and gives *either* social choices consistent with a social preference relation using the Condorcet criterion (RC3 and RC4) *or* social choices satisfying limited path independence (RC1 and RC3)

The collective

To show that the common members of two semidecisive sets D and E themselves form a fully decisive set, we adapt the preferences of table 3.4 to those of table 5.3. With preferences (R_i), everyone in D prefers b to c, so that $C(b,c) = \{b\}$ and everyone in E prefers c to a, so that $C(a,c) = \{c\}$. The form of the argument now depends on whether RC1 or RC4 holds.

(i)   RC1 implies $C(a,b) = \{b\}$.

(ii)   If each individual who is in both D and E switches in turn from R_i to R'_i, NM1 implies that the choice set from $\{a,b,c\}$ does not change from $\{b\}$; NM2 implies that the choice set from $\{a,b,c\}$ does not change from $\{b\}$ when those not in D change from R_i

Table 5.3 Preferences of intersecting fully decisive sets

| | preferences consistent with | |
individuals	I	II
in D and in E	$bP_icP_iaP_i$rest	$bP'_iaP'_i$rest
in D not in E	$aP_ibP_icP_i$rest	$R'_i = R_i$
in E not in D	$cP_iaP_ibP_i$rest	$aP'_ibP'_i$rest
others	$aP_icP_ibP_i$rest	$aP'_ibP'_i$rest

to R'_i. Since $C(a,b,c) = \{b\}$ by RC3, $C'(a,b,c) = \{b\}$. Then weak Pareto gives $C'(a,c) = \{a\}$. But a is not in $C'(a,b,c)$, so RC4 implies $C'(a,b) = \{b\}$.

In either case, the common members of D and E are semidecisive for a over b and theorem 5.1 implies that this set of people is fully decisive. The common members of all decisive sets of individuals therefore form a collective.

We have shown:

Theorem 5.2 There is a collective if there are at least three alternatives and the social choice rule satisfies
    choice from all subsets
    unrestricted preferences
    weak Pareto
    non-manipulability
and gives *either* social choices consistent with a social preference relation using the Condorcet criterion (RC3 and RC4), *or* social choices satisfying limited path independence (RC1 and RC3)

The dictator

The proof relating to dictatorship is exactly as in section 3.9 where we showed that RC2 is inconsistent with having more than one person in the collective. So:

Theorem 5.3 There is a dictator if there are at least three alternatives and the social choice rule satisfies
   choice from all subsets
   unrestricted preferences
   weak Pareto
   non-manipulability
and *either* RC2, RC3 and RC4 hold, *or* RC1, RC2 and RC3 hold

Therefore:

Theorem 5.4 There is a dictator if there are at least three alternatives and the social choice rule satisfies
   choice from all subsets
   unrestricted preferences
   weak Pareto
   non-manipulability
and if social choices are fully rational (so that they satisfy rationality conditions RC1 to RC4)

As we suspected, the dictatorship of Arrow's theorem remains when we replace independence by non-manipulability.

Oligarchy

In section 4.3 we showed that the collective is an oligarchy if social choices can be derived from a quasitransitive social preference relation using the Condorcet criterion (that is, if RC1, RC3 and RC4 hold). With non-manipulability, the oligarchy appears whenever we can use the Condorcet criterion (so that only RC3 and RC4 need hold). Suppose that for preferences (R_i), some individual j in the collective prefers a to all other alternatives in T, but that a is not chosen from T. The following argument shows that this is not possible if RC4 holds.

> RC4 implies that there is some alternative x in T for which $C(a,x) = \{x\}$.
> Consider the preferences (R'_i) for which $aP'_i x$ for any individual (including j) who holds $aP_i x$ and $xP'_i a$ for everyone else.
> Non-manipulability implies that $C'(a,x) = \{x\}$ (the only people who change their preference between a and x are those who are indifferent between a and x, and they clearly want x to be the sole choice when they change to R'_i).

So some set of individuals excluding j is semidecisive.
This contradicts the fact that j is in the collective.
So it cannot be true that a is not chosen from T.

We have shown that each member of the collective can ensure that his own most preferred alternative in T is in the choice set from T: the collective is an oligarchy (see Barbera 1976). We have proved:

Theorem 5.5 There is an oligarchy if there are at least three alternatives and the social choice rule satisfies
  choice from all subsets
  unrestricted preferences
  weak Pareto
  non-manipulability
and gives social choices consistent with a social preference relation using the Condorcet criterion (RC3 and RC4)

5.3 Maximin criterion for preferences

There is an alternative way of reaching a dictatorship from a collective which does not rely on RC2 – instead it uses the maximin criterion for deriving preferences about sets of alternatives from preferences about the alternatives themselves (see section 2.4). Consider preferences consistent with those of table 5.4, in which we suppose that the collective D^* has more than one member, one of whom is j. Since D^* is a collective, every semidecisive set includes all members of D^*, and so neither of the sets 'D^* except j' and 'others plus j' is semidecisive. Therefore $C(a,b) = \{a,b\}$, $C(a,c) = \{a,c\}$ and $C(b,c) = \{b,c\}$. So RC4 implies $C(a,b,c) = \{a,b,c\}$. With preferences consistent with column II, $C'(a,b) = \{a\}$ since D^* is semidecisive, and $C'(a,c) = \{a,c\}$, $C'(b,c) = \{b,c\}$ as before. Then RC3 implies that b is not in $C'(a,b,c)$, and RC4 gives $C'(a,b,c) = \{a,c\}$. However, by maximin, $\{a,c\}P_j\{a,b,c\}$, and so j has an incentive to state R'_j when he truly holds R_j: the rule is open to manipulation by j on $\{a,b,c\}$. So there cannot be anyone other than j in D^* (so that in column I everyone holds preferences consistent with $cP_ibP_iaP_i$rest), and j is a dictator. We have shown a result related to several in Pattanaik (1978, chapter 4):

Table 5.4 Preferences demonstrating dictatorship

individuals	restrictions on preferences	
	I	II
j	$cP_jbP_jaP_j$rest	$cP'_jaP'_jbP'_j$rest
other than j in D^*	$aP_ibP_icP_i$rest	$R'_i = R_i$
others	$cP_ibP_iaP_i$rest	$R'_i = R_i$

Theorem 5.6 There is a dictator if there are at least three alternatives, if individuals construct preferences using the maximin criterion and if the social choice rule satisfies
    choice from all subsets
    unrestricted preferences
    weak Pareto
    non-manipulability
and gives social choices consistent with a social preference relation using the Condorcet criterion (RC3 and RC4)

First preference rule

The proof of theorem 5.6 requires RC3 and RC4: it is not possible to show an equivalent result using RC1 and RC3. The first preference rule gives social choices that satisfy these conditions (see section 4.1) and no dictator. It is non-manipulable with maximin preferences as the following argument shows.

Suppose that a is one of i's most preferred alternatives and that, if i tells the truth, the choice set is C. For some reason, i tries to manipulate the first preference rule by pretending that a is not one of his most preferred alternatives (if he truly has no other most preferred alternative, he must promote some other or others). This pretence may:

(i)   Cause no change in the choice set (because of the preferences of other individuals). In this case i has no incentive to state a false preference.

(ii)   Exclude a from C, with no other change. By maximin, i prefers C to $C - \{a\}$, and so the falsehood leaves him worse off in this case.

(iii)   Include other alternatives in C without excluding a. These must
          be alternatives which are not truly amongst his most preferred
          (or they would be included in C when he tells the truth). By
          maximin, the resulting choice set is worse than C.

(iv)   Exclude a and include some others. The same argument as in (iii)
          applies.

He has no incentive to state the false preference in any of these cases.

5.4 Replacing weak Pareto

We can make a further refinement that extends theorems 5.1 to 5.6
somewhat – though it may not make them more useful in most contexts.
We can replace the weak Pareto condition with the less demanding
requirement of:

> **non-imposition**: for each pair of alternatives a and b there is some set
> of preferences for which $C(a,b) = \{a\}$

Suppose that non-imposition holds and $C(a,b) = \{a\}$ when individuals'
preferences are (R_i). Then, if every individual in turn changes his
preferences (if necessary) from R_i to R'_i so that aP'_ib, then the choice from
$\{a,b\}$ remains $\{a\}$. Otherwise an individual would have an incentive to state
R_i when he truly holds R'_i. So weak Pareto holds. Therefore in each
theorem we can replace weak Pareto with non-imposition; though there
are probably few circumstances in which we would not want a rule to
satisfy weak Pareto.

5.5 Resolute social choice rules

The various rationality conditions that we use place some structure on the
social choices that can occur – and one of the main ways in which the
proofs use rationality conditions is to rule out choice sets that contain
more than one alternative. In many electoral and public policy choices it
can be argued that we should impose this 'resoluteness' on the choice rule
directly – only one candidate wins an election, only one airport site is to
be chosen. If we do this, we find an inevitable dictator even without the
rationality conditions.

A social choice rule is **resolute** if each choice set contains exactly one
alternative. If we do not impose any rationality conditions, we cannot
deduce anything about, for example, $C(a,b,c)$ from $C(a,b)$. We can,

however, still proceed with proofs very much in the spirit of those that have gone before if, instead of considering $C(a,b,c)$, we consider $C(T)$ when everyone prefers a, b and c to all other alternatives in T. If we interpret the weak Pareto condition to say that b is not chosen from T if everyone prefers a to b, we know that $C(T)$ can only include a or b or c when everyone prefers these to all other alternatives. Similarly, instead of considering $C(a,b)$, we consider $C(T)$ when everyone prefers a and b to all other alternatives, so that only a or b can be chosen.

Table 5.5 Top-two semidecisiveness

individuals	restrictions on preferences
in D	aP_ibP_irest
others	bP_iaP_irest

In the same spirit, instead of considering semidecisiveness, we can conveniently examine sets of individuals who are **top-two semidecisive**: D is top-two semidecisive for a over b in T if $C(T) = \{a\}$ whenever preferences are as in table 5.5. With the amendment to top-two semidecisiveness, and concentrating on the choice from T, we can easily adapt our proofs to show that a resolute non-manipulable choice rule that satisfies the weak Pareto condition must give rise to a dictator. For example, to show that a set that is top-two semidecisive for a over b in T is top-two semidecisive for a over c in T, we consider preferences as in table 5.6. If D is semidecisive for a over b, a is chosen with preferences (R_i). As individuals change in turn from R_i to R'_i, b is always preferred by every individual to c, and so weak Pareto implies that the choice from T cannot change to c. If the choice changes to b when someone in D changes from R_i to R'_i, then he has an incentive to state R_i when he truly holds R'_i; if the choice changes to b when someone not in D changes from R_i to R'_i then he has an incentive to state R'_i when he truly holds R_i. So a is chosen with preferences (R'_i). If the choice changes from a to b or c when someone in D changes from R'_i to R''_i then he has an incentive to state R'_i when he truly holds R''_i; if the choice changes from a to b or c when someone not in D changes from R'_i to R''_i then he has an incentive to state R''_i when he truly holds R'_i. So a is chosen with preferences (R''_i), and D is top-two semidecisive for a over c in T. Note that we have not referred to any rationality condition.

Table 5.6 Resolute rules: preferences showing epidemic of top-two semidecisiveness

individuals	restrictions on preferences		
	(R_i)	(R'_i)	(R''_i)
in D	aP_ibP_irest	$aP'_ibP'_icP'_i$rest	$aP''_icP''_i$rest
others	bP_iaP_irest	$bP'_icP'_iaP'_i$rest	$cP''_iaP''_i$rest

By a series of similar arguments, we can show that there is a dictator at least when we are considering choices from the set T (which we have considered throughout by putting the relevant alternatives at the top of everyone's preferences). Without rationality conditions we cannot establish a formal link between choices from T and those from any other set of alternatives, and, in principle, there may be a different dictator when we consider choices from U than when we consider choices from T. To emphasise this, we say that there is a **fixed agenda** of feasible alternatives. Then we have:

Theorem 5.7 There is a dictator if there is a fixed agenda of at least three alternatives and a resolute social choice rule satisfies
   unrestricted preferences
   weak Pareto
   non-manipulability

As before, weak Pareto can be replaced by non-imposition and so we have:

Theorem 5.8 There is a dictator if there is a fixed agenda of at least three alternatives and a resolute social choice rule satisfies
   unrestricted preferences
   non-imposition
   non-manipulability

This theorem is usually known as Gibbard's theorem, or the Gibbard – Satterthwaite theorem (see Gibbard 1973, Satterthwaite 1975, Craven 1983).

Weakly resolute rules

A resolute social choice rule determines the single social choice whatever individuals' preferences may be. This seems somewhat unreasonable when everyone is indifferent between two alternatives, as a resolute rule must choose one of them. If $C(T) = \{a\}$ and everyone is indifferent between a and b, there is no preference information that we can use to separate a from b. This anomaly is avoided if the social choice rule is **weakly resolute**: if every individual is indifferent between a and b then b is chosen if and only if a is chosen, so that both or neither is chosen. In fact this weakening from resolute to weakly resolute makes no difference to our conclusion on the inevitability of a dictator, because we do not require any set of preferences in which everyone is indifferent between two alternatives to complete our proof. If a and b are both chosen, then they must be jointly most preferred by the dictator, whose power is therefore not reduced by the weaker condition. Thus we have:

Theorem 5.9 There is a dictator if there is a fixed agenda of at least three alternatives and a weakly resolute social choice rule satisfies
        unrestricted preferences
        non-imposition (or weak Pareto)
        non-manipulability

Weak resolution does not imply the use of a tie-breaker in an electoral system – weak resolution implies that, given universal indifference between some of the alternatives, the choice set may contain several alternatives. As long as everyone is indifferent between a and b, no-one will object if one of them is selected as the social choice (such as the Member of Parliament) by some random or arbitrary procedure, whereas the outcome of a tie-breaker that is used to select when preferences are evenly balanced between two or more alternatives may be important to many individuals who may then try to manipulate the outcome to use or avoid the tie-breaking procedure. For example, in first-past-the-post with an alphabetical tie-breaker, if 50 people hold cP_ibP_ia, 49 hold bP_iaP_ic and j alone holds aP_jbP_jc, then j has an incentive to say that his first preference is b, so that each of b and c gets 50 votes, and b wins on the tie-breaker. If j states his true preference, then c wins. In this case, j has an incentive to state an untrue preference in order to gain from the operation of the tie-breaker.

5.6 Further considerations

The results that we have so far achieved in this chapter make somewhat depressing reading for anyone who would like to find a democratic (or at least non-dictatorial) method of making social choices that avoids giving anyone the incentive to state an untrue preference. A fairly minimal rationality requirement gives an oligarchy, which becomes a dictatorship when individuals devise their preferences over sets using the maximin criterion. Alternatively, the requirement that the rule should always choose a single alternative also leads straight to dictatorship.

Random processes and proportional representation

A simplified version of Intriligator's (1973) social choice rule supposes that everyone is asked to state a single most preferred alternative, and that the choice of a single alternative is made by a random process in which the probability of choosing alternative a is proportional to the number of people who say that a is their most preferred alternative. The probability that a is chosen is:

$$n(a)/[n(a) + n(b) + ... + n(z)]$$

where $n(a)$, $n(b)$ ... are the numbers of people who say that a, b, ... is their most preferred alternative. A false statement that i most prefers b when he truly most prefers a increases the chance that b is chosen and reduces the chance that a is chosen – and therefore there is no incentive to state a false preference. Plainly also no-one is a dictator in this system – indeed, a minority group has some chance of securing its favoured outcome, although, of course, a large group of like-minded individuals has a greater chance.

Intriligator's scheme involves the use of a random process, and this may not be acceptable in a particular context. However, random processes are used to decide some issues; for example, the UK system of premium bonds, in which the interest on loans to the government is allocated at random, with the probabilities proportional to the number of bonds held.

Intriligator's method suggests one other context in which non-manipulable choices are possible. In a multi-party system, in which a number of parties have many candidates, Intriligator's scheme suggests that seats in Parliament be allocated in proportion to the number of first preferences for that party. In this form of proportional representation the same incentive to truth-telling applies as in Intriligator's random scheme.

A supporter of the Socialist party who votes for the Liberal party simply increases Liberal representation and reduces that of the Socialists. There can be no strategic reason for voting in opposition to one's most preferred party. I have suggested elsewhere (Craven 1984) a scheme for operating this method in a constituency based system – and for allowing individuals some choice between particular candidates within a party.

How easy is manipulation?

In many contexts, such as elections, an individual's incentive to state an untrue preference (to vote tactically) rests on his belief about how others will vote. Using first-past-the-post, the greatest temptation to vote tactically arises for someone who truly supports a candidate who is not expected to win, and who wants to elect whichever of the front-runners he dislikes least.

First-past-the-post is a special case of the **Borda score** in which each individual is asked to state strict preferences about all alternatives. Points are allocated to alternatives according to their place in each individual's preference order: if alternative a is in position t in i's preference order (so that i prefers $t-1$ alternatives to a), then a gains b_{it} points. These points are added, and the social preference relation then depends on the points allocated. For any individual $b_{it} \geqslant b_{iu}$ when $t < u$; the rule satisfies anonymity if $b_{it} = b_t$ for each i and each t, so that the points awarded are the same for each individual. Note that the outcome of the Borda score is unchanged if all the b_{it} are multiplied by some positive number, or if some number is added to all the b_{it}. So, if for every i and every t, $b'_{it} = \alpha b_{it} + \delta$ (where $\alpha > 0$), then the social preference relation using the b'_{it} is the same as that using the b_{it}.

First-past-the-post is a special case of the Borda score in which $b_1 = 1$ and $b_2 = b_3 = \ldots = 0$, and so the demonstration that first-past-the-post is manipulable is similar to that needed to show that the Borda score can be manipulated.

When there are three alternatives and the rule satisfies anonymity, all possible Borda scores can be obtained by setting $b_1 = 1$, $b_3 = 0$ and $b_2 = \beta$ where $0 \leqslant \beta \leqslant 1$ ($\beta = 0$ gives first-past-the-post). Suppose that i's preference is aP_ibP_ic. There are two circumstances where manipulation may be advantageous: first if the social preference relation when i states his true preference is $cPbPa$, and second if it is $bPaPc$.

If i states his true preference and the social preference is $cPbPa$, then:

$$\Sigma_c > \Sigma_b > \Sigma_a$$

(where Σ_a etc. are the total points allocated to each alternative), and i may have an incentive to state $bP'_iaP'_ic$ in order to give b more points, and so change the social preference to $bP'cP'a$. This will be successful if:

$$\Sigma_c - \Sigma_b < 1 - \beta$$

It is more likely to be successful if ß is small (close to first-past-the post). With a low value of ß, the strategy enhances b's position more than it does if ß is high.

If i states his true preference and the social preference is $bPaPc$, then:

$$\Sigma_b > \Sigma_a > \Sigma_c$$

and i may have an incentive to state $aP'_icP'_ib$ in order to give b fewer points in the hope of enhancing a's position (but without promoting c above a). Assuming that i has good reason to believe that $\Sigma_a - \Sigma_c > \beta$, then the manipulation is successful if $\Sigma_b - \Sigma_a < \beta$. This is more likely to be successful if ß is high.

So there is no clear answer on the relative potential for manipulability of the Borda score according to the values of the b_{it}. However, the circumstances in which manipulation is likely to be tempting are clear: first to try to ensure the choice (assuming only one is to be chosen) of the best of the front-runners, given that one's own favoured candidate is not likely to be a front-runner; second to reduce the chances of one's least favourite front-runners by putting them low in the stated preference.

In contrast to the relatively clear circumstances in which the Borda score can be manipulated, the method of **alternative vote**, though potentially manipulable, gives far less clear signals on the circumstances in which manipulation is likely to be beneficial. The alternative vote is a special case of the method of **single transferable vote** used for General Elections in some countries, including Eire, and proposed by many supporters of proportional representation in the UK. Every individual states strict preferences about the alternatives (in some versions, an individual need state preferences about only some of the alternatives) and every individual has one vote which is allocated initially to his most preferred alternative. At each stage of the process, votes may be reallocated amongst the alternatives as follows:

The alternative (x) with the fewest votes is eliminated and is no longer a 'remaining alternative'. The votes allocated to x are transferred to those of the remaining alternatives which are second most preferred by those who most prefer x. There is need for an appropriate tie-breaker if more than one alternative qualifies simultaneously for elimination.

Technically, this social choice rule is manipulable – though in practice this may be difficult to do (for a technical discussion, see Bartholdi, Tovey and Trick, 1989). Suppose that true preferences are as in table 5.7. If preferences are truthfully revealed, b is eliminated first as it gets 30 votes from B and C (compared to c's 31 from D and E), and then a is chosen with 51 votes from A and B to c's 49 from C, D and E. If one of the members of E who hold cP_ibP_ia instead states $bP'_icP'_ia$, c is eliminated first and b is chosen by 51 to 49. The member of E prefers b to a and so has an incentive to state R'_i when he truly holds R_i.

Table 5.7 Manipulability of the alternative vote

set of individuals	number of individuals	preferences
A	39	aP_ibP_ic
B	12	bP_iaP_ic
C	18	bP_icP_ia
D	10	cP_iaP_ib
E	21	cP_ibP_ia

The ability to manipulate this choice rule successfully depends on predictions of the order in which alternatives are eliminated, and on the subsequent allocation of second and subsequent (with more than three alternatives) preferences between the remaining alternatives. Manipulation in these circumstances may misfire if the prediction of the second or subsequent preferences is wrong, because changing the order of elimination can strengthen the position of an undesirable alternative.

We can say nothing definitive about the relative manipulability of choice rules, but the examples of this section show that, though non-dictatorial choice rules are generally manipulable, the possibilities for manipulation are not always as clear as they are with first-past-the-post or the Borda score.

Motivation and counter-threats

Our analysis of incentives to state a false preference has far reaching conclusions but is, in some ways, naive. Non-manipulability is a situation in which, if everyone else tells the truth, no single individual has an incentive to state a false preference. It is possible that a colluding group might have such an incentive, or that people might be dissuaded from stating a false preference by the possibility of counter-threats.

If i can change the choice set from $C(T)$ to $C'(T)$ by stating R'_i instead of his truly held R_i [and $C'(T)P_iC(T)$] he may not do so if he knows that j can change the choice from $C'(T)$ to $C''(T)$ by stating R''_j when i states R'_i where $C''(T)P_jC'(T)$ and $C(T)P_iC''(T)$. Individual i is dissuaded from stating R'_i to improve the outcome by the counter-threat that j can then change the choice set again to leave i worse off than if he had told the truth. We have presumed that i believes that j would do this only if j is made better off by his counter-threat than he is if he tells the truth whilst i does not [$C''(T)P_jC'(T)$]. In some discussions in the literature, i is more paranoid than we have supposed: he is dissuaded from false statements by a counter-threat that leaves i worse off than if he had told the truth, whether or not the counter-threat is better for j than stating the truth given that i states a false preference. So i fears a threat from j even if j would be made worse off by carrying out the threat. It seems more reasonable to suppose that counter-threats will be carried out only by those who gain by them than that they will be carried out whatever the cost to the individual making the counter-threat.

These more complex motivations, and the possibility of manipulation by colluding groups are beyond the scope of the arguments in this book – and take us quickly into the theory of games.

Implementation problems

The social choice analysis of this chapter examines the problem of getting people to state their true preferences. More general problems of implementation concern the possibility that people may not be asked to reveal their preferences, but to take some other action. If we want a 'truthful outcome' we must work out a procedure which, when it is **implemented**, the outcome is whatever it would be if everyone behaved according to their true preferences. A starting point for this analysis is the Clarke – Groves tax (see Sugden 1981) which is familiar to economists; further aspects of implementation problems are surveyed by Dasgupta, Hammond and Maskin (1979).

6

Rescuing majority voting

The voting paradox introduced in section 1.3 shows that majority voting 'does not work' in all circumstances. It is not possible to use majority voting and the Condorcet criterion when there are three or more alternatives because, for some combinations of preferences, the social preference relation involves a voting cycle such as aPb, bPc, cPa, so that $C(a,b,c)$ is empty. Arrow's theorem generalises this paradox to show that there are difficulties with any method that might be used to generate social choices.

One way of attempting to escape from the difficulties posed by Arrow's theorem is to examine the circumstances in which majority voting and the Condorcet criterion does not give a voting cycle, so that no social choice set is empty. If we remove the condition of unrestricted preferences so that we exclude consideration of combinations of preferences that give rise to the voting paradox, majority voting avoids dictators and is democratic to the full extent that each individual has equal weight in determining the social choice, and each alternative is treated equally with the other alternatives. To what extent must preferences be restricted to ensure that majority voting 'works'? Is it possible to describe the restrictions in ways that allow us to judge whether they are plausible.

6.1 Value restriction without indifference

We begin with the easiest case in which to consider majority voting. There are only three alternatives and there is an odd number of individuals, none of whom expresses any indifference. So there can be no tied votes: the social choice from any two alternatives is always a single alternative and, if we use the Condorcet criterion, the social choice from any set of alternatives is always a single alternative. Majority voting, in these circumstances, is resolute.

With three alternatives, there are six possible individual preferences: aP_ibP_ic, aP_icP_ib, bP_iaP_ic, bP_icP_ia, cP_iaP_ib, cP_ibP_ia. For simplicity of notation we refer to the number of people who hold aP_ib as $n(ab)$, the number who hold aP_ibP_ic as $n(abc)$, etc. A cycle arises if <u>all</u> of the following inequalities hold:

$$n(ab) = n(abc) + n(acb) + n(cab) > n(bac) + n(bca) + n(cba) = n(ba)$$
$$(6.1)$$

$$n(bc) = n(abc) + n(bac) + n(bca) > n(acb) + n(cab) + n(cba) = n(cb)$$
$$(6.2)$$

and

$$n(ca) = n(bca) + n(cab) + n(cba) > n(abc) + n(acb) + n(bac) = n(ac)$$
$$(6.3)$$

or if <u>all</u> of these inequalities hold with $<$ sign.

Adding inequalities 6.1 and 6.2 gives:

$$n(abc) > n(cba) \tag{6.4}$$

Adding inequalities 6.1 and 6.3 gives:

$$n(cab) > n(bac) \tag{6.5}$$

Adding inequalities 6.2 and 6.3 gives:

$$n(bca) > n(acb) \tag{6.6}$$

All of the inequalities 6.4, 6.5 and 6.6 must hold if 6.1, 6.2 and 6.3 all hold. If all the inequalities that are opposite to 6.1, 6.2, 6.3 hold, then so will three inequalities that have opposite inequality signs to 6.4, 6.5, 6.6:

$$n(cba) > n(abc) \tag{6.4'}$$
$$n(bac) > n(cab) \tag{6.5'}$$
$$n(acb) > n(bca) \tag{6.6'}$$

So, if there is a cycle, either 6.4, 6.5 and 6.6 all hold, or 6.4', 6.5' and 6.6' all hold.

One – but not the only possible – way of avoiding a cycle is that:

one of $n(abc)$, $n(bca)$, $n(cab)$ is zero, so that not all of 6.4, 6.5 and 6.6 hold

and:

one of $n(cba)$, $n(bac)$, $n(acb)$ is zero, so that not all of 6.4′, 6.5′ and 6.6′ hold.

These two conditions, each containing three possibilities, together give nine circumstances in which there can be no cycle. These circumstances appear in table 6.1. Every pair has some common feature: for example, if $n(abc) = 0$ and $n(acb) = 0$ then no-one has a as her most preferred alternative in $\{a,b,c\} - a$ is not 'first' for any individual. The nine cases of table 6.1 show all the possibilities of **value restriction** – there is some

Table 6.1 The nine possible value restrictions

	$n(abc) = 0$	$n(bca) = 0$	$n(cab) = 0$
$n(acb) = 0$	a not first	c not middle	b not last
$n(bac) = 0$	c not last	b not first	a not middle
$n(cba) = 0$	b not middle	a not last	c not first

alternative which everyone agrees is not in some position in their preferences. Any of these nine cases represents sufficient agreement to ensure the absence of a cycle of social preferences when majority voting is used.

Value restriction is a sufficient condition to avoid a cycle of preferences from three alternatives, and in one sense it is necessary too. If we know only which preferences exist, but we do not know how many people hold each preference, then we can guarantee to avoid a cycle only if we know that preferences are in some way value restricted. This is not difficult to demonstrate: if we know that some people hold aP_ibP_ic, some hold bP_icP_ia and some hold cP_iaP_ib, then it is possible that a cycle can arise (it does so if the numbers holding these preferences are roughly equal, and considerably greater than the numbers holding any other preference). So we have:

Theorem 6.1 If there are three alternatives, an odd number of individuals, no individual is indifferent between any two alternatives, and we do not know how many individuals hold each preference, then we can guarantee that social preferences are transitive using majority voting if and only if individual preferences are value restricted in some way

Single-peaked preferences

Historically, the first of these conditions to be examined in detail was that in which everyone agrees that some alternative is not last: for example, c is not last if $n(abc) = n(bac) = 0$ (see, for example, Black, 1948). This sort of agreement occurs when individuals have **single-peaked preferences**: it is possible to represent preferences diagrammatically, so that no-one's preferences come to more than one 'peak', when a more preferred alternative is represented by a higher point in the diagram. For example, figure 6.1 illustrates single-peaked preferences in which c is not

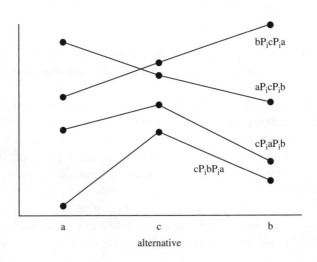

Figure 6.1 Single-peaked preferences

last in any of the individuals' preferences; figure 6.2 illustrates the preferences of three individuals who give rise to a cycle: the preferences of individual 1, (bP_1aP_1c) rise to two peaks – both a and b are above c. One individual of the three would have such double-peaked preferences whatever order we choose for the alternatives on the horizontal axis.

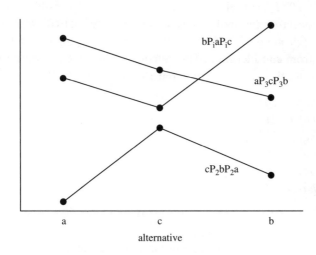

Figure 6.2 Preferences that give a cycle

An advantage of considering the restrictions in this way is that it may be possible to find some *a priori* justification for believing that preferences are single peaked. A usual example is that of political parties, which can be arrayed on the horizontal axis from 'left' to 'right' corresponding to the political meaning of these terms. Then it may be reasonable to suppose that preferences are single peaked: an individual is less favourably disposed towards a party that is far from her favourite on the Left–Right scale than towards a party that is nearer. This does not restrict anyone's first preference, but, if the three parties are Left, Right and Centre, then anyone whose most preferred party is Left has Centre as her second, as does anyone who most prefers Right. Preferences are single peaked because no-one puts Centre last.

It may be possible to devise an *a priori* justification for single-peaked preferences in other cases too: voting on public projects, for example, may have some feature such as size or cost or distance that can be put on the horizontal axis of a diagram in a way that everyone's preferences are single peaked.

Quasi-value restriction

Even if none of the conditions of value restriction can be applied directly, it may be possible to apply one of them after opposing preferences have been eliminated. For example, when majority voting is used, an individual who holds aP_ibP_ic cancels out the influence of one who holds cP_ibP_ia. So, suppose that as many individuals as possible are 'paired' with someone who has opposite preferences, and that all of these paired individuals are excluded from consideration. The outcome is unaffected and we would be left with only three types of preferences. For example, if:

$$n(abc) = 20$$
$$n(acb) = 21$$
$$n(bac) = 11$$
$$n(bca) = 16$$
$$n(cab) = 18$$
$$n(cba) = 24$$

then the 20 holding aP_ibP_ic would be paired with 20 of the 24 holding cP_ibP_ia, etc.

The numbers left after these eliminations are then:

$$n'(abc) = 0$$
$$n'(acb) = 5$$
$$n'(bac) = 0$$
$$n'(bca) = 0$$
$$n'(cab) = 7$$
$$n'(cba) = 4$$

After these eliminations the remaining preferences are single peaked: no-one puts c last (or b first), and so there is no voting cycle with the original preferences. In this case we are extending the idea of value restriction to quasi-value restriction: preferences are value restricted once all possible pairs of opposing preferences have been eliminated.

In the political example of single-peaked preferences, the extension to quasi value restriction allows that some people might hold the preferences LeftP_iRightP_iCentre and RightP_iLeftP_iCentre – as long as more people hold the opposite preferences with Centre as their first preference. Quasi value restriction therefore allows some diversity beyond single-peaked-ness.

An even number of individuals

An even number of individuals alters the outcome slightly, since tied votes are possible. However, by the same arguments as before, if preferences are value restricted and if a majority prefer a to b and a majority prefer b to c, then a majority prefer a to c. Strict social preferences are transitive.

Table 6.2 Intransitive indifference with an even number of individuals

individual	preferences
1	aP_1bP_1c
2	aP_2cP_2b
3	bP_3aP_3c
4	cP_4bP_4a

However the single-peaked preferences of table 6.2 show that statements involving social indifference need not be transitive.

In this example, $C(a,b) = \{a,b\}$, $C(a,c) = \{a\}$, $C(b,c) = \{b,c\}$, so that aIb, bIc and aPc. Hence, in the terminology introduced in section 4.3, the underlying social preference relation is quasitransitive, but not necessarily transitive. Note that this does not imply that there is an oligarchy (or any other concentration of power) – since any group of more than 50 per cent of the individuals is decisive, and no single individual can ensure the inclusion of her first preference in the choice set. The oligarchy result (theorem 4.4) fails because we are not allowing unrestricted preferences.

So, when there can be tied votes, strict social preferences are transitive, but statements of social indifference need not be so. Majority voting breaks down to the extent that social indifference may not be transitive, but there will still be a social choice set defined by the Condorcet criterion (in terms of the rationality conditions of chapter 2, the social choices satisfy RC1, RC3 and RC4). Theorem 6.1 becomes:

Theorem 6.2 If there are three alternatives, no individual is indifferent between any two alternatives, and we do not know how many individuals hold each preference, then we can guarantee that social preferences are quasitransitive using majority voting if and only if individual preferences are value restricted in some way

6.2 Preference restrictions with individual indifference

It is plain that any individual for whom aI_ibI_ic is irrelevant to the social statements between the alternatives $\{a,b,c\}$ – such an individual is said to be **unconcerned** about $\{a,b,c\}$. To apply value restriction in these circumstances, we need to adapt our definitions of 'not first', 'not middle' and 'not last' when people may be indifferent. We apply these definitions only to people who are not unconcerned.

Table 6.3 Preferences that are not value restricted

individual	preferences
1,2,3	aP_ibP_ic
4,5	cP_iaP_ib
6,7	bI_icP_ia

> z is **first** in $\{x,y,z\}$ for an individual if she does not prefer either x or y to z (so zR_ix and zR_iy)
>
> z is **middle** in $\{x,y,z\}$ for an individual if she does not prefer z to both x and y and if she does not prefer both x and y to z (so xR_izR_iy or yR_izR_ix)
>
> z is **last** in $\{x,y,z\}$ for an individual if she does not prefer z to either x or y (so xR_iz and yR_iz)

With the preferences of table 6.3, b is not first, c is not middle, a is not last in the preferences of individuals 1 to 5. However, for 6 and 7, b and c are first, a is last and b and c are middle and these preferences are not value restricted. Indeed, majority voting gives the cycle aPb, bPc and cPa.

Using these interpretations of value restrictions, it remains true that there can be no cycle if preferences are value restricted, but it is also possible to avoid a cycle in other circumstances. Consider, for example, the preferences of table 6.4. The 'positions' columns show that there is no value restriction: each alternative appears in each column. No cycle of the form bPa, aPc, cPb is possible because no one prefers b to a.

The social preference bPc occurs only if:

$$n_1 + n_4 > n_2 + n_3 + n_6 + n_7;$$

cPa occurs only if:

$$n_3 + n_6 > n_1 + n_2 + n_4 + n_5.$$

Adding these inequalities gives:

$$n_1 + n_4 + n_3 + n_6 > n_2 + n_3 + n_6 + n_7 + n_1 + n_2 + n_4 + n_5,$$

which requires:

$$0 > n_2 + n_7 + n_2 + n_5.$$

This is impossible, and so bPc and cPa cannot occur together, implying that the cycle aPb, bPc, cPa cannot occur. There can be no cycle, despite

Table 6.4 Preferences illustrating limited agreement

set of individuals	number of individuals	preference	positions		
			first	middle	last
E_1	n_1	aP_ibP_ic	a	b	c
E_2	n_2	aP_icP_ib	a	c	b
E_3	n_3	cP_iaP_ib	c	a	b
E_4	n_4	aI_ibP_ic	a,b	a,b	c
E_5	n_5	aP_ibI_ic	a	b,c	b,c
E_6	n_6	cP_iaI_ib	c	a,b	a,b
E_7	n_7	aI_icP_ib	a,c	a,c	b

the absence of all value restrictions. A cycle is effectively ruled out because there is agreement to the extent that no-one prefers b to a .

These preferences are an example of the condition of **limited agreement**: there are two alternatives x and y in the set of three such that no-one prefers x to y. The absence of a cycle when there is limited agreement is related to the conclusion on extended majority voting in section 4.4 that the sum of the required fractions for the social choices from $\{a,b\}$, $\{b,c\}$, and $\{a,c\}$ must exceed 2 in order to avoid a cycle of social preferences. In the example just given, the required fractions for the choices by majority voting from $\{b,c\}$ and $\{a,c\}$ are just over one half. To avoid a cycle, the required fraction from $\{a,b\}$ is 1, which is effectively satisfied because no-one prefers a to b.

When no-one is indifferent between alternatives, preferences that are in limited agreement are value restricted: limited agreement implies aP_ib for all i so that a cannot be last, nor b first. When there is individual indifference, limited agreement gives one set of conditions not covered by value restriction in which majority voting gives transitive or quasitransitive social preferences.

Finally, the condition of **extremal restriction** also suffices for majority voting to give transitive or quasitransitive social preferences. This condition requires that, if some individual k states aP_kbP_kc, then anyone who prefers c to a must hold cP_ibP_ia. So no individual can hold cP_iaP_ib, bP_icP_ia, cP_ibI_ia or cI_ibP_ia. If there are only strict preferences, extremal restriction excludes all but two preference patterns: for example, if aP_1bP_1c, then cP_iaP_ib and bP_icP_ia are excluded. If, in addition, aP_2cP_2b then bP_iaP_ic and cP_ibP_ia are excluded also. The example can be extended to show that there are no circumstances in which more than two different strict preferences are possible. Without individual indifference, extremal restriction is included in value restriction. When there is individual indifference, the preferences of table 6.5 satisfy extremal restriction, but

Table 6.5 Preferences that are extremal restricted but not value restricted

		positions		
individual	preference	first	middle	last
1	aP_1bP_1c	a	b	c
2	bP_2aI_2c	b	a,c	a,c
3	aI_3cP_3b	a,c	a,c	b

the preferences are not value restricted because each alternative is in each position for some individual.

Sen and Pattanaik (1969) have shown that we need look no further for restrictions on preferences that avoid a cycle of social preferences even when individuals express indifference between some alternatives:

Theorem 6.3 If there are three alternatives, and we do not know how many individuals hold each preference, then we can guarantee that social preferences are transitive or quasitransitive using majority voting if and only if the preferences of individuals who are not unconcerned are value restricted, extremal restricted or satisfy limited agreement

The scope of this theorem is limited to circumstances in which we know only the patterns of preferences, and not how many people hold each pattern. Obviously, if we know the numbers with each preference, there may be no cycle even if preferences are not value restricted, in limited agreement or extremal restricted. They may, for example, be unanimous, or quasi-value restricted.

More than three alternatives

When there are more than three alternatives, and no individual indifference for simplicity, it is necessary that individual preferences over each set of three alternatives should be value restricted – to avoid a cycle on those three alternatives. Fortunately, if preferences are value restricted on each set of three alternatives, then there can be no cycles on larger sets – social preferences cannot be, for example, aPb, bPc, cPd, dPe, ePa. The reason for this is that, if preferences are value restricted, strict preference statements are transitive, so that aPb and bPc imply aPc, cPd and dPe imply cPe, so that, if the cycle of five alternatives were to appear, there must also be a cycle on the three alternatives a, c and e. In this case, ruling out a cycle on sets of three alternatives rules out cycles on larger sets. So the full theorem proved by Sen and Pattanaik (1969) is:

Theorem 6.4 If we do not know how many individuals hold each preference, then we can guarantee that social preferences are transitive or quasitransitive using majority voting if and only if for every set of three alternatives, the preferences of individuals who are not unconcerned on that set are value restricted, extremal restricted or in limited agreement on that set of three alternatives

While this conclusion implies that we need not search for additional conditions to apply to larger sets of alternatives, it is worth remarking that a restriction on each set of three alternatives rules out many patterns of preferences. For example, suppose that there are four alternatives, b is not last in any set of three alternatives in which it appears, and d is not last in $\{a,c,d\}$. The only preferences that satisfy all of these restrictions are:

$$aP_ibP_idP_ic, \qquad bP_iaP_idP_ic, \qquad bP_icP_idP_ia, \qquad bP_idP_iaP_ic,$$
$$bP_idP_icP_ia, \qquad cP_ibP_idP_ia, \qquad dP_ibP_iaP_ic, \qquad dP_ibP_icP_ia$$

Only eight remain out of the 24 possible preferences over four alternatives (when there is no individual indifference). I know of no proof, nor of any counter-example, to the statement that if there are A alternatives, a restriction on each set of three implies that individuals can hold not more than 2^{A-1} preferences out of the possible total of $A!$ When $A = 3$, 4 preferences remain: $2/3$ of the logically possible total. If this conjecture is true when there are 6 alternatives, 32 preferences remain, which is fewer than 5 per cent of the 720 logically possible preference patterns. In this numerical sense, the restriction on the types of preferences (given that we do not know how many of each type there are) needed to ensure that majority voting gives no cycle would appear to become much more stringent as the number of alternatives increases.

The useful diagrammatic version of single-peakedness remains however many alternatives are considered – obviously if preferences over six political parties can be represented in a Left–Right spectrum, then preferences over any three of them can be similarly arrayed. In the appendix to this chapter we show that, when preferences involve no indifference, exactly 2^{4-1} preference patterns are possible if preferences about all A alternatives are single peaked. More generally, Sen (1970a) lists several papers on the probability of avoiding cyclical majorities.

Relation to Arrow's theorem

We have relaxed the condition of unrestricted preferences, and thereby avoided dictatorship. In our proof of Arrow's theorem, preferences are value restricted in tables 3.2 (b not last), and 3.3 (e not last). However, preferences in table 3.4 satisfy none of the conditions needed to avoid a cycle (the preferences of the first three sets of individuals can be used to construct a voting cycle). So, if preferences are value restricted, we cannot use the preferences of table 3.4, and it is not possible to show that the common members of any two fully decisive sets form a fully decisive set. Plainly, with majority voting, any set containing over half of the individuals is fully decisive, but any two sets of 51 per cent need have only 2 per cent of the total in common. These 2 per cent are not fully decisive, so that the common members of two fully decisive sets need not themselves be fully decisive. Majority voting does not give rise to a collective. This conclusion is consistent with the fact that the preferences used in table 3.4 can give a cycle.

6.3 Manipulability with restricted preferences

Majority voting is not manipulable when it gives no cycle: if i prefers b to a, then i's best chance of getting b chosen rather than a is to state a true preference for b over a. Majority voting satisfies pairwise independence, and therefore no other preference statement can affect the social preference between a and b.

When individuals' true preferences are value restricted, we need to consider what happens if an individual decides to state a false preference that is not value restricted in the same way, and this leads to a cycle. So, for example, it is important to know whether individuals who truly hold single-peaked preferences have an incentive to say that they hold such preferences so that majority voting can definitely avoid a cycle (see Pattanaik 1978, chapter 7).

To discuss this problem, consider the simplest possible case in which an odd number of individuals have preferences without indifference about three alternatives a, b and c. Suppose that alternative b is not last in any individual's preference so that true preferences are single peaked. The possible preferences and numbers of people who hold each are given in table 6.6. With these preferences, if aPb, then:

Table 6.6 Potentially manipulable single-peaked preferences

set of individuals	number of individuals	true preference
E	n_1	$aP_i bP_i c$
F	n_2	$bP_i aP_i c$
G	n_3	$bP_i cP_i a$
H	n_4	$cP_i bP_i a$

$$n_1 > n_2 + n_3 + n_4$$

and so aPc and alternative a is chosen. Individuals in E obviously have no incentive to change their preference, and since there are more in E than in F and G and H together, it does not matter what the others do. No-one has an incentive to state an untrue preference. The same analysis holds if c is chosen (because $n_4 > n_1 + n_2 + n_3$).

Complications occur if b is chosen:

bPa if $n_2 + n_3 + n_4 > n_1$
bPc if $n_1 + n_2 + n_3 > n_4$

People in F and G have no incentive to manipulate; those in E and H could state a false preference by putting b last and possibly lead to a voting cycle with a cycle of social preferences. The incentive to state such a false preference then depends on the outcome when there is a cycle of preferences (there can be a social choice, but not one derived from social preferences using the Condorcet criterion).

Suppose that someone in E states $aP'_i cP'_i b$ instead of her true preference $aP_i bP_i c$, and this gives a cycle. The incentive to do this depends on the choice set from $\{a,b,c\}$ and the way in which preferences about sets of alternatives are derived from preferences about the alternatives themselves. If the true preference is $aP_i bP_i c$ the maximin criterion (see section 2.4) gives:

$$\{a\}P_i\{a,b\}P_i\{b\}P_i\{a,c\}P_i\{a,b,c\}P_i\{b,c\}P_i\{c\}$$

Then i has an incentive to state $aP'_i cP'_i b$ if the social choice set from $\{a,b,c\}$ is either $\{a\}$ or $\{a,b\}$ as a result of the method use to resolve the voting cycle.

Perhaps the most obvious resolution when there is a cycle is that all three alternatives are chosen. Then the maximin method gives no incentive, and the voting rule is non-manipulable with maximin motivation. But perhaps this lack of resolution begs the question: majority voting makes no useful choice when there is a voting cycle, and so we must use some other method of making social choices when the voting paradox arises. Then someone in E can have an incentive to state an untrue preference if it is in her interest to bring this other method into use by causing a cycle to occur.

6.4 Support for majority voting

Majority voting has a strong intuitive appeal; we have examined restrictions on preferences that are needed to avoid cycles – and we have seen that these restrictions become more stringent as the number of alternatives rises. Majority voting can be supported on more formal grounds: plainly it satisfies weak Pareto (and strong Pareto) and independence. It also satisfies two conditions likely to be of great importance in an election and other circumstances of public choice, **anonymity** and **symmetry**.

Anonymity implies that every individual is treated in the same way: more formally, if two individuals exchange preferences, the result of the social choice rule does not change – the outcome of the rule does not depend on which individual expresses which preference, only on the number of individuals who express each particular preference. Symmetry implies that all the alternatives are treated in the same way – if every individual interchanges a and b in her preferences, then the social choice interchanges a and b (they swap places in the implied social preference relation). In addition, majority voting gives the fewest ties consistent with neutrality and anonymity – a is socially indifferent to b only if equal numbers hold aP_ib and bP_ia. Formally majority voting satisfies positive responsiveness: if initially a is socially indifferent to b (a tied vote), and then one person changes from aI_ib to aP'_ib, or from bP_ia to aR'_ib, whilst no-one else changes her preference, then a becomes socially preferred to b. It takes a change in only one individual's preferences to change from social indifference to social preference.

Anonymity, symmetry and independence require that the social choice between a and b is based only on $n(aP_ib)$ and $n(bP_ia)$, and so only a very limited class of social choice rules can satisfy these three conditions. This class includes the weak and strong Pareto extension rules and various forms of majority voting (including those involving majorities of more than 50 per cent that were discussed in chapter 4) – but these do not satisfy positive responsiveness, because they allow social indifference over a considerable range of values of $n(aP_ib)$ and $n(bP_ia)$. Thus (see May 1952 for a full proof):

Theorem 6.5 Majority voting is the only social choice rule that satisfies independence, positive responsiveness, symmetry and anonymity

Note that in May's formulation, independence and symmetry are combined into the condition of neutrality.

Individual preferences must be restricted to avoid the voting cycle, so that no social choice rule can satisfy unrestricted preferences, independence, positive responsiveness, symmetry and anonymity. We have seen (section 4.4) that extended majority voting can work with any set of individual preferences, and satisfies independence, anonymity and symmetry – and gives social choices that can be derived from a social preference relation (that is acyclic but not necessarily quasitransitive or transitive) using the Condorcet criterion. Though extended majority voting does not satisfy positive responsiveness, it does satisfy the much less demanding condition of non-negative responsiveness: if one individual's preference between a and b changes, the social preference between these does not change in the opposite direction.

The lesson of this chapter is essentially that majority voting is highly resolute in its choices between two alternatives (there is very little social indifference) but it can give rise to a voting cycle. The restrictions on preferences needed to ensure that there is no paradox become more stringent as the number of alternatives increases – the ratio of allowable preferences to logically possible preferences falls towards zero as the number of alternatives increases. On the other hand, extended majority voting can give no paradoxes, but is much less resolute – it gives social indifference in considerably more cases than majority voting. This failure to resolve issues with conflicting preferences becomes more widespread as the number of alternatives increase – the necessary majority tends towards unanimity as the number of alternatives increases.

It is a highly complex combinatorial problem (and one as yet unsolved as far as I know) to assess whether there are more circumstances in which majority voting gives a cycle, than there are circumstances in which extended majority voting does not give a unique choice from a set of alternatives. However, both these 'failures' are indications of the extent of the problem raised by Arrow's theorem – one shows that a particularly attractive choice rule – majority voting – cannot cope with many combinations of preferences; the other shows the cost in lack of resolution of any attempt to avoid the voting paradox by relaxing the condition of unrestricted preferences required by Arrow.

6.5 Limited agendas

We now turn to another possible route away from Arrow's dictator by exploring the possibility that a rule requires choice from a limited agenda of sets of alternatives rather than from all subsets. We saw in section 5.5 that, even with a fixed agenda (i.e. considering social choices from only one set of alternatives) a non-manipulable, resolute choice rule can be dictatorial. In this case, rationality conditions relating choices from different sets of alternatives are irrelevant. Also, assuming that the fixed agenda consists of all the alternatives, the independence condition is inoperative because there are no alternatives outside the set from which a choice is to be made.

If we interpret weak Pareto to be that a is not chosen from T if everyone prefers some other alternative in T to a, then the remaining conditions of Arrow's theorem are satisfied by first-past-the-post or the Borda rule. We know that these rules are manipulable, and even where manipulation is not a relevant consideration (as in ethical contexts for example), we may still be disturbed by the example illustrated by the preferences of table 6.7

Table 6.7 Borda score and independence

	preferences	
individuals	I	II
1,2	aP_ibP_ic	$aP'_icP'_ib$
3,4	bP_iaP_ic	$bP'_iaP'_ic$
5	cP_5bP_5a	$cP'_5bP'_5a$

when social choice is determined by a Borda score giving two points to the first alternative, one to the second and zero to the third in each individual's preference. In column I, a gets 6 points, b gets 7 points and c gets 2 points, so that b is chosen. In column II, a gets 6 points, b gets 5 and c gets 4 so that a is chosen. There is no change in individuals' preferences between a and b, yet in column I b is chosen and a is not while in column II a is chosen and b is not. The choice changes from b to a even though no-one's preference between a and b changes.

The potential problem illustrated in this example is, of course, simply another interpretation of an example showing how the Borda score fails independence. Denicolò (1987) surveys several results including that a dictator is inevitable with weak Pareto, unrestricted preferences and the requirement that the social choice from T shall not change from a to b if there is no change in any individual's preference between a and b. As in section 5.5, the rationality requirements were introduced indirectly by considering the choice from T when everyone prefers a and b to all other alternatives, which are then excluded by weak Pareto. This discussion of a fixed agenda therefore does not help in avoiding the dictator.

More extensive agendas

The previous paragraphs show that there is a dictator if the agenda is restricted to the set of all alternatives, and if we rule out the possibility that the social choice changes from a to b when there is no change in anyone's preference between a and b. However, it does not answer the question of how restricted the agenda must be (i.e. the sets of alternatives for which the rule must work) to avoid a dictator if we maintain weak Pareto, unrestricted preferences, independence (in its Arrow form) and rationality conditions appropriate to the sets of alternatives remaining on the agenda. If the choice rule does not give choices from all pairs of alternatives, we cannot use RC1 to RC4, but we can use the Greek-named rationality conditions introduced in the appendix to chapter 4:

> **Condition α**: if U is a subset of T, a is chosen from T and a is in U, then a is chosen from U (if T contains only two alternatives, then α is RC3)
>
> **Condition ε**: if U is a subset of T, then $C(T)$ is not a proper subset of $C(U)$
>
> **Condition β**: if U is a subset of T, a and b are both chosen from U and a is chosen from T then b is also chosen from T

Suppose that there are four alternatives $\{a,b,c,d\}$, and the agenda is restricted so that the social choice rule gives a choice from the set of all four alternatives and from every set of three alternatives – but not from sets of two alternatives. As with a fixed agenda, we can show how the rule seems to choose from a pair of alternatives even if that pair is not in the

Table 6.8 Implicit choices satisfy RC1

stage	preferences	choice from	choice set	why
1	(R_i^{ab})	$\{a,b,c,d\}$	$\{a\}$	by assumption
2	(R_i^{bc})	$\{a,b,c,d\}$	$\{b\}$	by assumption
3	(R_i^{ab})	$\{a,b,d\}$	$\{a\}$	α and ε from 1
4	(R_i^{abc})	$\{a,b,d\}$	$\{a\}$	independence from 3
5	(R_i^{bc})	$\{b,c,d\}$	$\{b\}$	α and ε from 2
6	(R_i^{abc})	$\{b,c,d\}$	$\{b\}$	independence from 5
7	(R_i^{abc})	$\{a,b,c,d\}$	$\{a\}$	α from 4 & 6
8	(R_i^{abc})	$\{a,c,d\}$	$\{a\}$	α and ε from 7
9	(R_i^{ac})	$\{a,c,d\}$	$\{a\}$	independence from 8
10	(R_i^{ac})	$\{a,b,c,d\}$	$\{a\}$	α and ε from 9

agenda by constructing preferences (R_i^{ab}) from (R_i): in R_i^{ab} individual i has the same preference between a and b as in R_1, but promotes a and b so that she prefers them to all other alternatives.

We use similar conventions for constructing R_i^{abc} in which i prefers a, b and c to all other alternatives, and so on.

We say that a is implicitly chosen from $\{a,b\}$ with preferences (R_i) if a is chosen from $\{a,b,c,d\}$ with preferences (R_i^{ab}). If these implicit pairwise choices satisfy pairwise independence, RC1 and RC3 there is a collective; add RC2 and the inevitable dictator emerges.

Pairwise independence of these implicit choices requires that, if each individual's preference between a and b is the same in R_i as in R'_i, then the choice from $\{a,b,c,d\}$ with preferences (R_i^{ab}) is the same as the choice from $\{a,b,c,d\}$ with preferences $(R_i'^{ab})$. The argument runs as follows:

(i)   Independence implies that the choice from $\{a,b,c\}$ with preferences (R_i^{ab}) is the same as the choice from $\{a,b,c\}$ with preferences (R'^{ab}_i) (note that both R_i^{ab} and R'^{ab}_i put a and b in the same order, and a and b before c).

Weak Pareto and rationality conditions α and ε imply both the following:

(ii)   the choice from $\{a,b,c\}$ with preferences (R_i^{ab}) is the same as the choice from $\{a,b,c,d\}$ with preferences (R_i^{ab}), and

(iii)   the choice from $\{a,b,c\}$ with preferences (R'^{ab}_i) is the same as the choice from $\{a,b,c,d\}$ with preferences (R'^{ab}_i) .

Therefore the choice from $\{a,b,c,d\}$ with preferences (R_i^{ab}) is the same as the choice from $\{a,b,c,d\}$ with preferences $(R_i'^{ab})$ and pairwise independence of the implicit choices follows. The stages of the arguments to show that RC1 to RC3 hold for the implicit choices are shown in tables 6.8 to 6.10. In each table the column labelled 'why' shows how each line is justified.

For RC1 we must show that, if the choice from $\{a,b,c,d\}$ with preferences R_i^{ab} is $\{a\}$ and the choice from $\{a,b,c,d\}$ with preferences R_i^{bc} is $\{b\}$, then the choice from $\{a,b,c,d\}$ with preferences R_i^{ac} is $\{a\}$. The stages of the argument are given in table 6.8.

To show that implicit choices satisfy RC2 we must show that if the choice from $\{a,b,c,d\}$ with preferences (R_i^{ab}) is $\{a,b\}$ and the choice from $\{a,b,c,d\}$ with preferences (R_i^{bc}) is $\{b,c\}$, then the choice from $\{a,b,c,d\}$ with preferences (R_i^{ac}) is $\{a,c\}$. The stages of the argument are given in table 6.9.

Table 6.9 Implicit choices satisfy RC2

stage	preferences	choice from	choice set	why
1	(R_i^{ab})	$\{a,b,c,d\}$	$\{a,b\}$	by assumption
2	(R_i^{bc})	$\{a,b,c,d\}$	$\{b,c\}$	by assumption
3	(R_i^{ab})	$\{a,b,d\}$	$\{a,b\}$	α and ε from 1
4	(R_i^{abc})	$\{a,b,d\}$	$\{a,b\}$	independence from 3
5	(R_i^{bc})	$\{b,c,d\}$	$\{b,c\}$	α and ε from 2
6	(R_i^{abc})	$\{b,c,d\}$	$\{b,c\}$	independence from 5
7	(R_i^{abc})	$\{a,b,c,d\}$	$\{a,b,c\}$	α and β from 4 & 6
8	(R_i^{abc})	$\{a,c,d\}$	$\{a,c\}$	α from 7
9	(R_i^{ac})	$\{a,c,d\}$	$\{a,c\}$	independence from 8
10	(R_i^{ac})	$\{a,b,c,d\}$	$\{a,c\}$	α and ε from 9

To show that implicit choices satisfy RC3, we must show that if a is chosen from $\{a,b,c,d\}$ with preferences (R_i), then a is chosen from $\{a,b,c,d\}$ with preferences (R_i^{ab}). The stages of the argument are given in table 6.10.

After showing that RC1 and RC3 implicitly hold, we can demonstrate the existence of a collective. With RC2 as well, the inevitable dictator ensues.

The crucial feature of this example is that, by taking a suitable selection of feasible sets and preferences, we can show an implicit choice from pairs of alternatives. More generally, the crucial condition for this sort of stage-by-stage argument is that the agenda is restricted in such a way that it allows implicit pairwise choices: every pair of alternatives is the in-

Table 6.10 Implicit choices satisfy RC3

stage	preferences	choice from	choice set	why
1	(R_i)	$\{a,b,c,d\}$	includes a	by assumption
2	(R_i)	$\{a,b,c\}$	includes a	α from 1
3	(R_i^{abc})	$\{a,b,c\}$	includes a	independence from 2
4	(R_i^{abc})	$\{a,b,c,d\}$	includes a	α and ε from 3
5	(R_i^{abc})	$\{a,b,d\}$	includes a	α from 4
6	(R_i^{ab})	$\{a,b,d\}$	includes a	independence from 5
7	(R_i^{ab})	$\{a,b,c,d\}$	includes a	α and ε from 6

tersection of two or more sets on the agenda. In our example, $\{a,c\}$, which is not on the agenda, is the intersection of $\{a,b,c\}$ and $\{a,c,d\}$ which are both on the agenda.

We have shown that there is a dictator with four alternatives: we could run through a similar (albeit considerably longer) argument with more alternatives, to demonstrate:

Theorem 6.6 There is a dictator if there are at least four alternatives, the agenda is restricted but allows implicit pairwise choices and the social choice rule satisfies

> **unrestricted preferences**
> **independence**
> **unanimity**

and if social choices satisfy rationality conditions α and ß

(Note that if α and ß hold, then so does ε: see the appendix to chapter 4)

Appendix: Counting single-peaked preferences

Proof that, if there are A alternatives, all preferences are single peaked and there is no individual indifference, then exactly 2^{A-1} preferences are possible.

The alternatives are numbered from 1 to A (in the political example, alternative 1 could be the most left wing candidate and alternative A the most right wing). Let $H(m,A)$ be the number of single-peaked preference patterns possible with alternative m as the most preferred alternative, and A alternatives altogether. We are looking for a formula for $H(1,A) + H(2,A) + .. + H(A,A)$. Plainly $H(1,A) = 1$ (the preference coincides with the numerical order of the alternatives) and $H(A,A) = 1$ (preferences coincide with the reverse numerical order). For $m \neq 1$ and $m \neq A$, either alternative $m-1$ or $m+1$ is second most preferred because preferences are single peaked. If we exclude alternative m, then alternatives $m-1$ and $m+1$ are in positions $m-1$ and m respectively in a list of $A-1$ alternatives. So:

$$H(m,A) = H(m-1, A-1) + H(m, A-1).$$

We can use this recursive relation to find $H(m,A)$: $H(1,1) = 1$; $H(1,2) = H(2,2) = 1$; $H(1,3) = 1$, $H(2,3) = H(1,2) + H(2,2) = 2$, $H(3,3) = 1$. We are in fact constructing Pascal's triangle:

$$H(1,1)$$
$$H(1,2) \qquad H(2,2)$$
$$H(1,3) \qquad H(2,3) \qquad H(3,3)$$
$$H(1,4) \qquad H(2,4) \qquad H(3,4) \qquad H(4,4)$$
$$H(1,5) \qquad H(2,5) \qquad H(3,5) \qquad H(4,5) \qquad H(5,5)$$

in which each entry is the sum of the two entries diagonally above it [for example, $H(3,5) = H(2,4) + H(3,4)$]. Numerically, we have:

$$
\begin{array}{ccccccccc}
 & & & & 1 & & & & \\
 & & & 1 & & 1 & & & \\
 & & 1 & & 2 & & 1 & & \\
 & 1 & & 3 & & 3 & & 1 & \\
1 & & 4 & & 6 & & 4 & & 1 \\
\end{array}
$$

$$1 \quad 5 \quad 10 \quad 10 \quad 5 \quad 1$$

etc.

In Pascal's triangle, $H(m,A) = (A-1)!/[m! \times (A-m-1)!]$, and the sum of entries in any row is $H(1,A) + H(2,A) + ... + H(A,A) = 2^{A-1}$, thus proving the result.

7

Rights

Arrow's theorem is the consequence of attempts to find a satisfactory alternative to majority voting that avoids the voting paradox. The theorems that we have met in the last four chapters demonstrate that all social choice rules have their drawbacks – generally, those proposed violate independence (or give incentives not to tell the truth), or do not give rational social choices in some defined sense, or, like majority voting, they do not 'work' for some combinations of individual preferences.

Even beyond these objections, it is possible that a social choice rule such as majority voting gives undesirable outcomes even in circumstances where it works. For example, the unrestrained use of majority voting may be objectionable because a majority might choose an alternative that has severe effects on a minority; it is an all-too-frequent lesson of history that minorities have suffered at the hands of majorities (the opposite happens too, and is equally covered by what follows). People have different views of what constitutes an individual's **rights** – ranging from the right not to suffer physical harm through to the libertarian economic view that people have the right to keep – and hence not be taxed on – their income and wealth. A majority can out-vote any individual and so no individual right would be safe if all social choices were determined by the view of a majority.

7.1 Imposed social choices

To protect rights, we might want to modify the operation of a social choice rule. First, we consider the consequences of **imposing** some social choices by preventing the choice of a particular alternative whatever individual preferences may be. For example, it may be considered wrong that I take heroin: it would be wrong for me to choose to do so, and it would be wrong for any other group (a collective, for example) to force me to do so. Therefore any alternative that involves me taking heroin cannot be chosen (we assume that some feasible alternative does not involve me taking heroin). This resolution is not likely to cause any great difficulty for the technical operation of a social choice rule if it satisfies the independence condition: if some alternative is not to be chosen from T, then the rule can be applied to those alternatives in T that can be chosen. If the rule does not satisfy independence, it is possible that the presence of an unchoosable alternative affects the choice from the remainder (this would be the case if the rule were the Borda score, for example, in which the points given to an unchoosable alternative affect the points given to other alternatives).

There is obviously scope for argument on the justification for an imposed ban on choice in the contexts of economic or political decisions. How might one justify banning a candidate in an election? How offensive must the views of an individual or his party be before he cannot be a candidate? What is the best lower age limit for election candidates? What criteria might be used to rule out an airport site or a freeway route before individuals are asked their preferences? Why should people be banned from taking drugs, or owning firearms, or driving without a seat belt? Fortunately, we need not discuss these questions in the context of social choice rules – we need merely note that they are the questions that lie behind imposed aspects of the social choice process.

In individual ethical judgements, these arguments are internal to the person making the judgement. He judges – independent of the preferences of others, and independent also of his own interests – that he cannot approve some alternatives. If he is unconditionally opposed to the use of the death penalty, he will not approve an execution even if he, and every one else whom he cares about, would be much safer if a particular individual were dead. If he is opposed to working on the Sabbath, then he does not approve certain actions even if they make him much more comfortable. If he disapproves of taxation, he may prefer to starve for the want of social security, and feel that this is better than violating his strongly held principles. These are personal judgements – whose origins again fall outside the scope of social choice theory, but not, of course of more general moral discussion.

7.2 Rights to choose

A second way of protecting rights is to restrict the operation of the social choice rule to ensure that some choices reflect only the preferences of those who are most closely concerned. An individual's choice of clothes, or hairstyle, or entertainment, for example, may be regarded as his own decision whatever views others may have on what he does.

More difficult questions might arise when we consider an individual's choice on how he spends his income. If the individual is small in the economic sense that his choice of what to buy does not affect the prices paid by others, nor their job prospects, then we could argue that he should be able to decide what he buys and where he works. On the other hand, if his choices affect other people because he bids up the prices of what he buys, or his actions reduce the sales of a product so that some people lose their jobs, then we might argue that he should not be free to choose what he does and that the social choice rule should take account of the consequences for others.

However we might resolve these particular examples, it is safe to assume that most people regard some issues as an individual's own concern – and so, as social choice theorists, we can examine the consequences of these individual rights and the extent to which several individuals' rights may, or may not, be compatible.

In a formal analysis, we can specify rights in a variety of ways:

R1   Individual k has the right to ensure that a is not chosen from any set in which a appears with other alternatives. This is most likely if alternative a contains some feature that particularly affects k.

R2   Individual k has the right to determine the choice set from $\{a,b\}$ – so that $C(a,b) = \{a\}$ if aP_kb, $C(a,b) = \{b\}$ if bP_ka. This is most likely to be justified when the difference between alternatives a and b is some issue that is considered to be solely the personal concern of k – such as his clothes or his choice of entertainment. Indeed, the alternatives could be described in detail, identifying features of the alternatives that are the private business of a particular individual. There may also be features that are no-one's private business. In economic examples, the features private to individual k could be his own consumption of goods; features that are no-one's exclusive private business could include the provision of public goods such as national defence.

R3   Individual k has the right to exclude a or b (but not both) from
            the choice set from any set that contains both a and b. In this
            example, a and b might differ in some way that primarily affects
            k, and he is allowed to make the decision on which one shall be
            excluded from consideration in determining the social choice.

R2 and R3 can be related to one another according to the rationality of
social choices. For example, if k has the right to determine $C(a,b)$ (version
R2), he would effectively have the right to prevent the choice of one of a
or b from a larger set if choices satisfy rationality condition RC3. If he
excludes a from $C(a,b)$, then RC3 implies that he cannot choose a from
any set that also contains b.

Rights assignment

To examine the effect of rights in the context of social choice we consider
a **rights assignment** in society which describes the rights that each
individual has. A rights assignment describes the rights of each individual,
and is an additional input to the social choice process. Obviously two
rights in an assignment could, in principle, conflict: we cannot have an
assignment in which both i and j have a right to choose from $\{a,b\}$, for
example. We assume that the rights assignment is **coherent**: that is, rights
themselves do not conflict.

Note that the question of rights is perhaps most likely to arise in an
ethical context in which the social choice rule is an individual's way of
making judgements. So the judging individual decides on the rights
assignment, and it is up to him to ensure that it is coherent. This may not
be easy: the following example shows that lack of coherence may not be
immediately obvious.

Gibbard's wall colours: all alternatives excluded

Gibbard (1974) gives an example in which all alternatives might be
excluded because externalities between individuals (each cares what the
other does) involve a fundamental disagreement. Each of two individuals
h and k can each paint his own bedroom walls one of two colours, yellow
and white. So the four alternatives are: $a = (y,w)$, $b = (y,y)$, $c = (w,y)$,
$d = (w,w)$ (where in obvious notation (w,y) implies h's walls are white, k's
are yellow), and one of these four is to be implemented. Individual h has
the right to choose between alternatives that differ only in the colour of his

own walls, that is between a and d and between b and c; similarly k has a right to choose between a and b and between c and d. Individual h prefers that the walls are the same colour, and *ceteris paribus h* prefers that his own walls are white rather than yellow; individual k prefers that the walls are different colours, and *ceteris paribus k* prefers that his own walls are white rather than yellow. So their preferences are as in table 7.1.

Table 7.1 Preferences in wall-colour example

individual	preferences
h	$dP_h bP_h cP_h a$
k	$aP_k cP_k dP_k b$

The exercise of h's rights eliminates a (because $dP_h a$) and c (because $bP_h c$), and the exercise of k's rights eliminates b and d (because $aP_k b$ and $cP_k d$), so that every alternative is excluded from $C(a,b,c,d)$. The assignment of rights seems *prima facie* reasonable, but the opposing preferences lead to a problem.

The lesson of this example is that an apparently reasonable assignment of rights may not be coherent: the exercise of the rights may exclude every alternative. One interpretation of this example is that h and k would be perpetually repainting their walls because there is no equilibrium from which neither wants to change. In an economic context, we could get round the externality if h were prepared to accept a payment not to repaint his walls yellow if k chooses yellow. However, this sort of side-payment is not within the context of the problem that we have specified in which a, b, c, d are the only four outcomes possible.

7.3 Rights and Arrow's theorem

The main difficulty with any rights assignment can be found in the proof of Arrow's theorem. If an individual can determine the social choice from one pair of alternatives, if the rule satisfies independence and weak Pareto and social choices satisfy RC1 and RC3, then that individual is a dictator. Note that we do not even need RC2, because RC1 and RC3 imply a collective and the right ensures that the collective has only one member. So a single right over an innocuous choice concerning an individual's own lifestyle can, in the context of Arrow's theorem, lead to dictatorial power over all issues.

Worse still, perhaps, is the consequence of the fact that there cannot be two dictators. Thus if Arrow's other conditions hold, the rights assignment cannot give each of two individuals the right (version R2) to determine the choice from a pair of alternatives. Sen (1970b) has narrowed down the range of conditions needed to produce this impossibility. There are two cases to consider, depending on the rights assignment:

(i) k has the right to determine $C(a,b)$ and h has the right to determine $C(b,c)$. Thus the two rights involve a common alternative b. Suppose that cP_kaP_kb, bP_hcP_ha and everyone else prefers c to a. The rights assignment gives $C(a,b) = \{a\}$, $C(b,c) = \{b\}$ and, if RC1 holds, $C(a,c) = \{a\}$. Alternatively, if RC3 holds, $C(a,b,c) = \{a\}$ and a is in $C(a,c)$. However, everyone prefers c to a, so that the two rights plus the use of either of the rationality conditions RC3 or RC1 are inconsistent with weak Pareto.

(ii) k has the right to determine $C(a,b)$ and h has the right to determine $C(c,d)$. The two rights do not involve a common alternative.

Suppose that $dP_kaP_kbP_kc$, $bP_hcP_hdP_ha$ and everyone else prefers b to c and d to a. The rights assignment gives $C(a,b) = \{a\}$, $C(c,d) = \{c\}$; weak Pareto gives $C(b,c) = \{b\}$ and $C(a,d) = \{d\}$. If RC1 holds, then $C(a,b) = \{a\}$ and $C(b,c) = \{b\}$ gives $C(a,c) = \{a\}$, whilst $C(c,d) = \{c\}$ and $C(a,d) = \{d\}$ gives $C(a,c) = \{c\}$. These two conclusions are inconsistent. Alternatively, RC3 cannot hold whatever alternatives are in $C(a,b,c,d)$.

We need only one of the rationality conditions and we do not use independence in this proof: the conditions under which two rights and weak Pareto are inconsistent are very undemanding. The result is:

Theorem 7.1 If a social choice rule satisfies unrestricted preferences and weak Pareto, and if two individuals each have rights over a (distinct) pair of alternatives, then the choices given by the rule cannot satisfy either RC1 or RC3

Note that this is a very similar result to that of section 4.4 on extended majority voting. Suppose that there are $n \geqslant 2$ individuals and 3 alternatives, and that the rights assignment allows i to choose from $\{a,b\}$ and j to choose from $\{b,c\}$. So the required fractions for the social choices between a and b and between b and c are $1/n$. To avoid a cycle, the sum of the required fractions must exceed 2, and so the required fraction for the choice between a and c must exceed $2-2/n$ and so exceeds 1. Since $2-2/n \geqslant 1$, even a unanimous choice between a and c does not avoid the cycle.

Sen points out that this is a very alarming result. The Pareto condition is very attractive – if social choices do not reflect unanimous views, then it is hard to ask for any relation between individual preferences and social choices. On the other hand, a rights assignment involving only two rights is nearly as simple as possible. Yet these two conditions are sufficient to violate basic collective rationality conditions.

Lady Chatterley's Lover

Sen's motivation for the preferences used in this example is a fine example for the social climate of the 1960s, but may be a little tame for modern-day consumption. A copy of *Lady Chatterley's Lover* (once banned in unexpurgated form in the UK, subject of a famous censorship trial in 1960) is available:

> individual h is a 'prude', and c is the alternative that h reads the book
> individual k is 'lascivious' and a is the alternative that k reads the book
> b is the alternative that neither reads the book

(Note that we exclude the possibility that they both read the book. Consider if you prefer who gets the last seat to see a pornographic play).

The prude prefers that no-one reads the book, but, if anyone does so, he prefers to do so to avoid the corrupting and depraving influence on the other, who is, in the prude's opinion, already more than sufficiently depraved (so bP_hcP_ha). The lascivious prefers that the prude should read it to broaden his mind, but if he does not read it, k prefers to read it himself rather than have no-one read it (so cP_kaP_kb). Each has the right to decide whether or not he himself reads the book. So h has the right to determine $C(b,c) = \{b\}$; k has the right to determine $C(a,b) = \{a\}$. RC3 implies that $C(a,b,c) = \{a\}$, and so a is chosen from $\{a,c\}$, even though both individuals prefer c to a. Alternatively, RC1 implies $C(a,c) = \{a\}$ again violating weak Pareto. The exercise of rights leads to the choice of a, and there is another alternative c which everyone prefers to a.

This example demonstrates Sen's devastating result that just two individuals with very minimal rights, one of two basic rationality requirements and the weak Pareto principle are not compatible. In these circumstances, we might contemplate dispensing with the rationality condition, but this gives us very little scope for relief from the difficulty. We need to use RC3 only because of the way in which we have specified the rights (version R2) and the Pareto principle. If we use the R3 version of rights, and modify slightly the definition of the weak Pareto condition, the problem remains even without the rationality conditions. If k's right over a and b and h's right over b and c are version R3, then, in the *Lady Chatterley* example, the rights of k and h ensure that neither b nor c is chosen from $\{a,b,c\}$ – so that a must be chosen. This choice conflicts with a version of weak Pareto that states that a is not chosen from $\{a,b,c\}$ if everyone prefers some other alternative (in this case c) to a. In this formulation, there is no mention of rationality conditions.

An economic example

The liberal view of free-market economics provides another example of the potential conflict between rights and Pareto. The free-market mechanism can be considered as a social choice rule which operates as follows:

(i)   An alternative is defined by the amount of each good held by each individual.

(ii)   Individuals are free to choose what to demand and supply within the constraints of their given resources and the prices that determine their budget constraints.

(iii)   The market mechanism uses these choices to determine prices at which these demands and supplies balance.

The choice rule gives the market-clearing alternative (supply = demand for all goods) as the chosen alternative. Basic welfare economics teaches that, in certain conditions, the market-clearing alternative is Pareto Optimal – no other alternative exists which is preferred by all (or by some with none opposed) to the market-clearing alternative. The combination of each individuals' right to choose subject to a budget constraint rules out Pareto-inferior outcomes.

However, one of the 'certain conditions' needed for this conclusion is that there are no externalities between individuals' preferences. An externality occurs if, for example, one individual's preferences depend in part on the goods that another individual has. If such externalities occur, the market mechanism – the exercise of rights of freedom of choice – chooses an alternative that is not Pareto Optimal: there is some other feasible outcome which everyone prefers (see, for example, Varian, 1987).

The economic example and the *Lady Chatterley* example both illustrate the conflict of rights with the Pareto condition. Both arise because there are externalities in preferences: in the economic example, some individuals' preferences depend on what others consume. In the *Lady Chatterley* example, each has preferences about the other's reading and not just about his own.

7.4 Sacrificing the Pareto condition

We have seen that we cannot in all circumstances respect rights without violating the Pareto condition. One or other must have precedence. Most supporters of individuals' rights would probably argue that rights have a greater priority than any social choice that is determined from a combination of several people's preferences: rights are there to protect people from the potentially damaging consequences of choices based on the views of many people. So, since the Pareto condition is a rule which makes social choices according to the views of everyone, it is secondary to the rights of individuals, and would be sacrificed when Pareto conflicts with rights.

The actual outcome of the social choice process implied by a market economy is likely to involve respect for rights (which determine individuals' own choices) and may give an outcome which is, in fact, inferior to some other potential outcome by weak Pareto. Thus, in this case, satisfying Pareto is secondary to the exercise of rights.

Liberal individuals: ineffective preferences

In an ethical context, the social choice rule under consideration is an individual's own way of forming judgements given his own and others' preferences. The judging individual makes the rights assignment, and then (assuming that it is coherent) makes judgements according to that assignment. If he then finds that this rights assignment and others' preferences imply aPb, even though everyone (including himself) prefers b to a, he may decide that his own preference for b over a should be ineffective in determining the judgement. He cannot include bP_ia and the rights assignment. So when we are considering a judgement by an individual who wants to respect rights and would normally want to obey

the Pareto condition, we have a straightforward resolution of the conflict
if he decides that his own preferences will not be effective when they
conflict with the exercise of others' rights. Effectively, the Pareto condition
is sacrificed to maintain individuals' rights.

For example, in the *Lady Chatterley* example, the liberal, who is
forming his judgement and who is neither the prude nor the lascivious,
might privately prefer that the prude should read the book rather than the
lascivious (perhaps because he too is fed up with the prude's overbearing
ways, and would like him to have a broader education). However, he does
not want his preference for c over a to be effective in the determination of
the social choice because he wants to respect the rights assignment and the
preferences of the prude and the lascivious. Thus, in making his liberal
moral judgement, he ignores his private view of what is good for the
prude.

7.5 Limiting rights

The alternative way of resolving a conflict between rights and the Pareto
condition involves limiting the exercise of rights. Are there circumstances
in which people's rights should not be respected? We report here two
attempts to provide reasonable criteria for limiting the exercise of rights.
In fact neither seems particularly satisfactory.

Restricting the rights of the meddlesome

In the *Lady Chatterley* example, each individual disagrees with the other
on what the other prefers to do – each exhibits an externality. Indeed, it
can be argued (see Blau 1975) that the prude's preference for b over a (that
he should not read the book given that the lascivious does not read it) is
stronger than his preference for b over c (that he, rather than the lascivious
should read the book if someone is going to do so). This 'intensity of
preference' is not an invocation of cardinal utility, but based simply on the
fact that $bP_h cP_h a$ so that c comes between b and a. Using any reasonable
measure of the intensity of preference, his preference for b over a is
stronger than his preference for b over c. The prude is **meddlesome**
because:

(i)   his preference about the pair on which the other has a right is
        stronger than his preference about the pair where his own right
        applies, and

(ii)   he does not agree with k on the pair for which k has a right.

Similarly, the lascivious individual (k) is meddlesome, because cP_kaP_kb. His preference for c over b (on which h has a right) is stronger than his preference for c over a (to which his own right applies). Also, he does not agree with h on the pair of alternatives over which h has a right.

It might be argued that, by stating meddlesome preferences about issues that concern others, an individual forfeits the right to enforce the choice on issues that concern him alone. An individual deserves the protection of rights only when he respects the rights of others. Then, in the *Lady Chatterley* example, both individuals forfeit their rights, so that cPa by the weak Pareto principle, and some other aspect of the choice rule must determine the remaining social preferences.

The use of meddlesome preferences to remove rights implies that the social choice rule violates independence: an individual has a right involving two alternatives unless his and others' preferences over other alternatives show him to be meddlesome. Sen (1976), Suzumura (1978) have argued that this is not a very liberal way out of the conflict between Pareto and rights because the protection of freedoms is <u>most</u> needed in circumstances where others might meddle – so that these are precisely the circumstances when rights should be upheld. In addition, individuals may differ in the range of issues to which they wish rights to apply – and some rights may be more important than others. So, I might disagree with your preference on a matter which I do not think to be very important, and this disagreement might cause me to forfeit my rights on other matters which I think are much more important. A failure to be aware of another's preference on a relatively trivial matter is a poor basis for losing the right to life.

Another criticism is that Blau has not demonstrated why an individual's rights, rather than some other aspect of his preferences, should be forfeit when he is meddlesome. In the *Lady Chatterley* example, individuals 1 and 2 both prefer c to a essentially because they are meddlesome, and Sen (1976) argues that these preferences should be ignored in the determination of social choices, rather than those for the individuals' 'self-regarding' pairs. In the *Lady Chatterley* example, if h is meddlesome, then he must prefer c to a: he prefers that he reads the book himself rather than k doing so, even though he does not want to read it himself, and k does want to read it. So, if we ignore both individuals' preferences for c over a , then a is chosen through the exercise of rights. This decision respects each individual's desire to read the book. With this solution, the social choice rule takes no account of the externality aspects of preferences (the market mechanism in which individuals are free to choose their own supplies and demands similarly ignores externalities) and reflects only the self-regarding parts of preferences.

More than two people

A fundamental logical problem with limiting the rights of the meddlesome is that it does not resolve the problem of conflict between rights and Pareto when there are more than two people. For example, suppose that h has a right of type R3 over (a,b), k has a similar right over (b,c), and j over (c,d) and that preferences are as in table 7.2.

Table 7.2 Pareto-rights conflict with more than two people

individual	preferences
h	$dP_haI_hcP_hb$
k	$bP_kdP_kaP_kc$
j	$cP_jbP_jdP_ja$

If the rights are exercised, none of b, c or d can be chosen from $\{a,b,c,d\}$. However, everyone prefers d to a, so that the rights conflict with an unanimous preference. No individual expresses a meddlesome preference as Blau defines it since no-one has an unambiguously stronger preference concerning someone else's pair than his own. Each individual expresses externalities in his preferences, and the 'liberal' choice that respects rights but ignores externalities (and ignores Pareto) is a.

The attempt to solve the rights problem by limitation when people exhibit meddlesome preferences seems neither satisfactory nor, in certain cases, logically sound.

Alienable rights

An alternative attempt to resolve the Pareto-rights conflict is put forward by Gibbard (1974), who examines the consequences of making rights alienable. People may indeed choose not to exercise their rights if that option is open to them. If i has a right of type R3 over a and b, and aP_ib, then i has the right to insist that b is excluded from the choice set from any set that also includes a. However, if there is some other individual right over a and c that results in the exclusion of a from the choice set, i might choose not to exercise his right to exclude b if he prefers b to c. In the *Lady Chatterley* example:

(i)   the prude (h) has the right to exclude c (that the prude reads the book) or b (that neither reads the book): bP_hcP_ha,

(ii)   the lascivious (k) has the right to exclude a (that the lascivious reads the book) or b (that neither reads the book): cP_kaP_kb.

If the lascivious exercises his right according to his preferences, he would exclude b. If the prude need not exercise his right, he would not do so. By exercising it he excludes c, leaving a as the chosen alternative. He prefers c to a, as does the lascivious, so the unanimous choice is c. Therefore the prude would choose not to use his right in these circumstances.

Gibbard's general formulation is slightly different from this. It requires that i's right is not exercised if this would avoid a cycle of social preferences given that all other rights are exercised and unanimous judgements made. Suppose, for example, there are four alternatives and two individuals:

(i)   individual i has a right to exclude either a or b; $dP_iaP_ibP_ic$

(ii)   individual j has a right to exclude either c or d; $bP_jcP_jdP_ja$.

Unanimous preferences exclude a (both prefer d to a) and c (both prefer b to c). If i and j were to exercise their rights, they would exclude b and d, leaving no alternative in the choice set. Under Gibbard's scheme, these rights would become ineffective. Once again the Pareto condition takes precedence over the exercise of rights – which would be contested by those who believe that individual rights are more worthy of respect than any collective judgement – even a unanimous one.

Rights and manipulability

In a moral judgement, the judging individual does not take account of alienated rights because they and the Pareto condition are in conflict. Our use of the *Lady Chatterley* example suggests that the lascivious and the prude are actually using the social choice mechanism to decide what is to happen: they are making a public choice. In this latter context, individuals may indeed choose whether or not to exercise their rights in the same way that they might choose to state an untrue preference. If the prude were actually to announce that he would prefer to read the book than to leave it unread, thus stating an untrue preference cP_hbP_ha, then the exercise of rights would exclude only alternative b that neither reads the book. Then the Pareto condition would determine that the prude should read the book. In problems of public choice, an individual's decision on whether or not to exercise his right is a strategic one.

Theorem 5.1 points to a further potential difficulty. Suppose that we consider only the exercise of rights and unanimous judgements (that is, the weak Pareto condition). Suppose that all rights are of type R2 (defined over pairs of alternatives), and that the rights assignment itself is coherent. Then, using Gibbard's criterion for not exercising a right, we define a social choice rule as follows:

(i)   If a is in T, then a is in $C(T)$ if there is no b in T such that either everyone prefers b to a or that an exercised right over $\{a,b\}$ excludes a from $C(a,b)$.

(ii)   A right over $\{a,b\}$ is exercised only if there is no T including both a and b which would have an empty choice set using (i).

Note that a right may be exercised for one set of individual preferences and not for some other set. Note also that if (i) would give an empty choice set for T, then no right affecting a pair of alternatives in T is exercised.

Then:

(i)   The rule satisfies choice from all subsets and unrestricted preferences, by virtue of (ii) above.

(ii)   It satisfies weak Pareto.

(iii)   The social choices are consistent with a social preference relation using the Condorcet criterion. RC3 holds: if a and b are in T and a is in $C(T)$, then not everyone prefers b to a, and, if an individual exercises a right over $\{a,b\}$, then that individual prefers a to b. Hence a is in $C(a,b)$. RC4 holds: if a is in $C(T)$ and a is in $C(a,b)$ then a is not excluded from $C(T \cup \{b\})$ by a unanimous judgement or by an exercised right.

(iv)   An individual i who has a right over $\{a,b\}$ is semidecisive for a over b (the right would be exercised if, for example, aP_ibP_i others and everyone else prefers b to a to all other alternatives).

So, by theorem 5.1, either the rule is manipulable or i is fully decisive – that is, he is a dictator. As there cannot be more than one dictator, there cannot be more than one person with rights. We know from the *Lady Chatterley* example that there cannot be more than one person with rights if we want to avoid a social preference cycle, given that rights are always exercised in accordance with true preferences. We have now shown that, even if rights are not exercised when they help cause cycles, the result of having more than one person with rights is that the rule is in some way manipulable.

If the rule is manipulable, there is some combination of preferences which gives some individual an incentive to state a false preference. This false preference will have one of the following effects:

(i)   It will bring into effect a right or a unanimous judgement and thereby avoid a social preference cycle that would otherwise occur, thus ensuring that some other right can be exercised.

(ii)   It will bring into effect a right or a unanimous judgement to create a social preference cycle to avoid the exercise of other people's rights.

8

Justice

Many people – even those who have liberal views about rights and freedoms – would argue that social justice involves caring about others, and particularly involves caring about the less well-off members of society. How can we formally incorporate this concern for justice into the theory of social choice? What principles of justice can be used consistently in the formation of judgements?

8.1 Impersonal principles of justice

For most of this chapter, we regard principles of justice as impersonal. We are not concerned with the well-being of a particular named individual but we can be concerned with impersonal descriptions of positions that individuals are in, such as the worst-off person or the one at the median of an income distribution. If there are n people in society, then each alternative description of society contains n positions.

An intellectual experiment for making such impersonal judgements is put forward by Rawls (1971, who justifies a particular view of justice which we discuss later). His argument is that principles of social justice should be determined behind a 'veil of ignorance'. Imagine that you are designing an ideal society of which you will be a member, but you do not know which member you will be. If 'designing a society' seems odd, think less ambitiously of designing a tax-and-benefit system. The veil of ignorance implies that the rule is derived independent of individual interests. You are not allowed to design society (or the tax-and-benefit system) to protect your own vested interests, neither is the rule justified on the basis of compassion for your own friends and relations or hatred of your enemies. The design of a just system therefore is based on the positions that people can be in (specified, for example, by an anonymous list of individual incomes) but without knowing which individual is in which position.

Alternative justifications for impersonal principles of justice include the golden rule of moral philosophy 'do to others as you would have done to you', or one of the few pieces of verse regularly quoted by social choice theorists (to show that they have read Arrow 1951 who quoted it first, rather than the tombstone on which it is alleged to have been inscribed):

> Here lies Martin Engelbrodde,
> Ha'e mercy on my soul, Lord God,
> As I would do were I Lord God,
> And thou wert Martin Engelbrodde

However we justify impersonality, we suppose that an individual constructs a principle of justice as follows. She has preferences about the n individual positions in each alternative, where the positions in each alternative can be numbered arbitrarily. We read the phrase $[a,i]P_k[b,j]$ as 'individual k prefers position i when alternative a occurs to position j when alternative b occurs'. Indifference statements involving I_k and preference-or-indifference statements involving R_k can be made similarly.

8.2 Status rankings

The individual wants to use these preferences about the positions within alternatives to make statements about the justice of particular alternatives. As we shall see, these may be relative statements 'a is more just than b' or inclusive '$J(T)$ is the set of most just alternatives within the set T'. If she expresses preferences R_i over all possible $n.A$ positions in the A alternatives, we can say that she has n different rankings of the alternatives by arguing as follows. For each alternative, find from R_i the position that is most preferred (choose arbitrarily if some are indifferent and preferred to all others). The first relation between the alternatives is then the order of preference given by R_i between all of these best positions. Then do the same with the second best positions, and so on to the worst positions. This then gives n rankings of the alternatives derived from R_i. For example, with $n = 3$ and $A = 4$, suppose that her preferences are:

$$[a,1] \ P_i$$
$$[b,3] \ P_i$$
$$[a,2] \ P_i$$

$$[c,1]I_i[c,2]\ P_i$$
$$[d,3]\ P_i$$
$$[b,2]I_i[d,1]I_i[c,3]\ P_i$$
$$[d,2]\ P_i$$
$$[a,3]\ P_i$$
$$[b,1]$$

(i)   the best positions in each alternative are $[a,1]$, $[b,3]$, $[c,1]$ (or $[c,2]$), $[d,3]$; so the first ranking of the alternatives puts a first, b second, c third, d fourth.

(ii)   the second best positions are $[a,2]$, $[c,2]$ (or $[c,1]$), $[b,2]$ and $[d,1]$; so the second ranking puts a first, c second and b and d joint last (because $[b,2]I_i[d,1]$).

(iii)   the worst positions are $[c,3]$, $[d,2]$, $[a,3]$, $[b,1]$ so that the third ranking puts c first, d second, a third and b last.

She has one ranking of the alternatives for each level or status between best-off and worst-off, and so we call them **status rankings**. The important point about status rankings is that they have similar characteristics to the preferences of n individuals, though they are in fact all derived from one person's preferences about all the possible positions in all alternatives.

Parallel with Arrow's theorem

First, consider a Pareto-like rule: alternative a is considered to be more just than b if all the status rankings put a above b. This can be extended to a stronger version in which some status ranking places a above b, and no status ranking places b above a (this extension is like that from weak to strong Pareto). This impersonal Pareto-like principle is very similar in form (though not quite in definition) to the **grading principle** introduced by Suppes (1966). Therefore we refer to it (in the strong form, allowing for indifference) as the impersonal grading principle.

The impersonal grading principle in this form does not perhaps have the immediate appeal of the Pareto condition in other contexts, because the impersonal environment prevents us from saying that a is more just than b when each individual is better off in a than in b. Even if a is more just than b according to the impersonal grading principle, it remains possible that, when individuals have been assigned to positions, some people are better off in b than they are in a (some specified individual might prefer her position in b to that in a; this does not contradict the possibility that the best position in a is preferable to the best position in b and that the worst position in a is preferable to the worst position in b). Another possible reason for rejecting the impersonal grading principle is that we would want to judge the <u>relative</u> merits of positions within an alternative. For example, an individual might base her view of justice on the distribution of income (using a Gini coefficient or some other measure of distribution), and believe that a reasonably equal distribution is better than a very unequal one. Then she would say that a distribution of £20 to one person and £25 to the other is better than £21 to one and £35 to the other, even though the latter would be considered more just using the impersonal grading principle.

A second possible condition that might be used in constructing a principle of justice has similarities to the condition of independence. This condition states that if R_i and R'_i give the same status rankings between a and b, then R_i and R'_i lead to identical statements on the justice of a and b. This principle is appropriate only when the individual has no view on how much more preferable $[a,j]$ is than $[b,k]$ – that is, when her preferences are ordinal. In the context of Arrow's theorem, we argued that it may be possible to get only ordinal information on n individuals' preferences; it seems a less persuasive argument in the current context as all the preference information that we are using here concerns the individual's own views of the merits of different positions, and she may well be able to consider her own intensity of preferences. We return to this issue in the next chapter.

If we accept the impersonal grading principle and the independence condition, we can draw an immediate lesson from Arrow's theorem. In Arrow's theorem, the social choice rule converts n individual preferences into social choices; in the present context, a principle of justice converts preferences over all positions in all alternatives into justice statements about the alternatives. However, the preferences over positions give rise to n status rankings, and the independence condition implies that if two preferences give identical preference rankings, then they lead to the same justice statements. Therefore we can think of a principle of justice as a mechanism for converting n status rankings into justice statements.

Assuming that a principle of justice must be usable with any preferences that the individual may state (unrestricted status rankings), and that we want to make transitive statements about justice (so that if a is judged to be more just than b, and b is more just than c then a is more just than c, and similarly for 'indifference' statements of equal justice) we have an exact parallel with Arrow's theorem. Our impersonal grading principle is analogous to the strong Pareto principle, and so the parallel is with the version of Arrow's theorem that allows for a hierarchy of dictators (theorem 3.10). If the first dictator in the hierarchy is indifferent, social choices may follow the preferences of the second in the hierarchy and so on. In our present context, a 'dictator' is not a named individual but a status, such as the best position or the median position in each alternative. So we have a theorem that has similarities to that of Arrow, but is applicable in a context where an individual is trying to determine the relative merits of particular states of society in an impersonal way:

Theorem 8.1 If a principle of justice gives transitive statements about the relative justice of alternatives and satisfies unrestricted preferences, the impersonal grading principle and independence then there is a hierarchical dictatorship of statuses

8.3 Maximin and leximin

Theorem 8.1 tells us that one status is 'dictatorial' (with a possible subsequent hierarchy), but does not specify which this status is. In his *Theory of Justice* Rawls (1971) uses the veil of ignorance argument to justify both the impersonality of justice, and the view that the lowest status should have this dictatorial role. Behind the veil of ignorance, an individual is attempting to design a principle of justice to judge society, without knowing which position any individual will occupy. If she designs a very inegalitarian society, there is a chance that she will be one of the very poor people – and a chance that she will be one of the very rich. If she designs a society in which everyone has entirely equal incomes, no-one will be better or worse off than she is, but this common income level may not be very high because people need the chance to become rich (or the threat of being poor) to make them work hard and increase national income. Rawls argues that, faced with this problem, people will be cautious and make sure that the worst position is as good as possible. Between all the principles of justice that one might design, Rawls argues that people choosing behind the veil of ignorance will choose the system whose worst-off position is as well-off as possible. So they choose a principle of justice in which the lowest status is first in the hierarchy of 'dictatorial' status rankings.

If Rawls' principle is applied to sharing out a national income of fixed size, it naturally implies that everyone has an equal share. However, in economic contexts, the incentive argument implies that some inequality may well remain to provide the stimulus to make national income bigger.

Under Rawls' principle, any policy that causes inequality can be justified only if the worst position is better than is the worst position when there is complete equality.

Rawls calls this the **difference principle**; it is more usually known as the maximin rule (maximise the minimum position). In Rawls' theory, it is the second of two principles: the first principle is that every individual should have the maximum liberty that is consistent with similar liberty for everyone else. Furthermore, the first principle is applied before the second: Rawls would not sacrifice liberties to make the worst position better. Plainly Rawls' first principle leads to a practical question of the maximum extent of liberty consistent with like liberties for others. Our previous chapter tells us that even not very extensive liberties or rights can cause serious problems in social choice. However, the purpose of this chapter is not to discuss liberties and rights, but to concentrate on the implications of the maximin principle. So we presume that the maximin principle of justice is applied only to those alternatives that do not violate liberties protected by Rawls' first principle.

The maximin rule can be extended to allow a hierarchy to deal with cases in which the individual is indifferent between the worst positions in a and b. Then the judgement between a and b is made on the basis of the second worst position in each; if these are also indifferent, take the third worst position, and so on. This is known as lexicographic maximin (or **leximin** to save space).

The most frequent criticism of Rawls' justification of maximin arises from observed decision-making. In most decisions that involve uncertainty, people are cautious, but not usually to the extreme extent implied by this argument. In economics, attitudes to risk are defined by relating the expected (or average) outcome from an uncertain prospect to the outcome of a certain prospect. An individual is risk averse if she prefers a certain prospect with outcome Y to an uncertain prospect whose average outcome is Y (for example, a prospect that gives a probability of 0.25 of getting $5Y/2$ and a probability of 0.75 of getting $Y/2$). The extent to which she is risk averse is measured by the minimum certain outcome that she would accept rather than face the uncertain prospect. Someone whose minimum is $3Y/4$ is more risk averse than someone whose minimum is $4Y/5$.

Rawls' justification of maximin implies very great risk aversion. If the worst position in alternative a gives an income of $Y/2$ (and, for the sake of argument, we suppose that income is all that anyone cares about), then Rawls presumes that the individual prefers alternative b in which everyone gets slightly more than $Y/2$. This is true even if in a only one person gets $Y/2$, and everyone else gets very much more. If nine people get $10Y$, and one gets $Y/2$, the average expected outcome of a for any individual who is behind the veil of ignorance is $(9 \times 10Y + Y/2)/10 = 9.05Y$. However, Rawls would prefer an alternative in which everyone gets $0.51 Y$ to this alternative, because the worst position is marginally better, even though the average position is considerably worse. In practice, people do not seem to be as risk averse as this sort of example implies.

Perhaps the best answer to the criticism that Rawls assumes that people are very risk averse is that most empirical evidence comes from choices that are much more restricted than those envisaged by Rawls. Behind the veil of ignorance, people are judging nothing less than life patterns. The worst-off person has the least desirable living standard (judged by whatever criteria are most relevant) and no hope of improvement. She has no hope of remission from this worst position, and we might argue that people are much more likely to be risk averse when contemplating their whole life than they are in less general circumstances.

Alternative justification of leximin

If we believe that a principle of justice must satisfy the conditions specified in theorem 8.1 (unrestricted preferences, grading, independence and transitive justice statements), then there is a hierarchy of dictatorial statuses. Further, the epidemic proposition tells us that, if there is some circumstance in which the worst status ranking determines the principle of justice, then it does so in all circumstances (except when it gives indifference).

Suppose, for example, that $[a,1]P_i[b,2]P_i[b,4]P_i[a,3]$ and that i is indifferent between $[a,3]$ and all other positions. Now if it were to happen that individual j was in position 1 in alternative a, and in position 2 in alternative b, and that individual k was in position 3 in alternative a and position 4 in alternative b, then the **Sen—Hammond equity axiom** (see Hammond 1976) argues that individual k's position should be made as good as possible, since j is in a preferred position to k in both alternatives. Given that $[b,4]P_i[a,3]$, the equity axiom implies that b is better than a. In this example, the second status ranking determines relative justice of a and b rather than the first. Note that the axiom can be used only when individuals are assigned to positions in certain ways: if instead j was in $[a,1]$ or $[b,4]$ and k was in $[b,2]$ or $[a,3]$ then the axiom would have nothing to say since j is better off in a and k is better off in b. However, if the lower status ranking determines the outcome in one circumstance, the epidemic proposition implies that it does so in all circumstances. By extension, the worst status is the first in the dictatorial hierarchy, the second worst is next and so on. So leximin is justified by finding some circumstance in which it is considered reasonable, and then using the epidemic proposition to show that leximin must always be used. We might remark, however, that this justification shows the power of the epidemic proposition rather than the necessary desirability of leximin.

8.4 Less demanding principles of justice

The parallel with Arrow's theorem suggests an alternative approach to principles of justice. In the context of social choice, we have seen that there is a collective if we insist on Arrow's conditions with a requirement of path-independent rather than transitive social choices.

To discuss path independence in the context of justice requires that the principle of justice makes a choice to parallel the social choice set of earlier chapters. This occurs if the principle divides a set of alternatives into those that are chosen as just and those that are deemed to be unjust. In separating the just from the unjust, we are not putting alternatives in order of relative justice and using this to find the most just alternative(s) in any set.

Path independence requires that we can find the just alternatives in set S by dividing it into T and U, choosing the just alternatives from T and U, and then choosing the just alternatives from the combined set of just alternatives in T and in U. That is, if $J(X)$ is the set of just alternatives in X, then path independence gives $J(S) = J(T \cup U) = J[J(T) \cup J(U)]$. The parallel with the collective of individuals that arises with path independent choices implies that there is a collective of status rankings with the following properties:

(i)   If a is better than b according to all rankings in the collective, then b is not in the set of just alternatives from any set of alternatives in which a and b both appear.

(ii)   No smaller set of status rankings can be guaranteed to exclude an alternative from the set of just alternatives.

So, for example, a principle of justice might say that, when a and b are both available, b is not in the set of just alternatives if, and only if, each of the five worst positions in a is better than the corresponding position in b.

This principle gives path independent justice statements (the 'collective' is the five worst positions) – sacrificing the full transitivity of leximin in order to avoid the great emphasis placed on the worst position.

8.5 Personal principles of justice

The principles of justice that we have discussed so far are all impersonal – they consider positions within alternatives without knowing which individual holds which position. Some discussions involve principles of justice that are not impersonal, and are concerned with the preferences of individual k about the positions of individual i (not necessarily the same as k) in an alternative. So $[a,j]P_k[b,i]$ is to be read as 'individual k prefers the position of individual j in alternative a to the position of individual i in alternative b'. The three individuals (or any two of them) could be identical: if $i = j = k$ then k is making a preference statement about her own positions in the two alternatives. Individual k is presumed to use statements of this kind to determine her own views of the relative justice of the various alternatives.

An individual who has preferences about the positions of specified others may devise her preferences on several bases. She might personalise her preferences using her own feelings about other people ('I like alternative a because my friend j does well in it' 'I like b because that dreadful i does badly in it'). However, if we are contemplating a theory of justice that is independent of such personal feelings, we may support a liberal-sounding principle that k respects i's own preference between $[a,i]$ and $[b,i]$: each individual regards other individuals as the best judges of their own self-interest. Individual k might argue that the best evidence she has on the relative merits of $[a,i]$ and $[b,i]$ is i's own preference between these. Then $[a,i]P_k[b,i]$ if and only if $[a,i]P_i[b,i]$. If every individual always uses this principle, the **axiom of identity** is said to hold. The axiom of identity is sometimes justified on the grounds of 'doing to others as you would have them do to you': you (k) would not want another (i) to prefer $[a,k]$ to $[b,k]$ if you in fact prefer $[b,k]$ to $[a,k]$, therefore you do not say that $[b,i]P_k[a,i]$ if $[a,i]P_i[b,i]$. There may, of course, be occasions when k passionately believes that i is not the best judge of what is better for herself, and then the axiom of identity fails – essentially because k's passionate beliefs override any liberal tendencies.

The axiom of identity obviously places some restrictions on the diversity of individuals' preferences, but this will be limited to the extent that individuals have different views on who is best off, second best, etc.

in each alternative. Suppose that, in addition to the axiom of identity, everyone agrees on the relative position of each individual in each alternative: in alternative a, everyone agrees who is best-off, who is second-best, ..., who is worst-off, and similarly in each other alternative. To what extent does this agreement, together with the axiom of identity, imply that individuals have similar preferences over the alternatives? Would, for example, agreement in these areas mean that preferences about alternatives are single peaked or otherwise value-restricted? Then majority voting could be used consistently to determine a social choice given that each individual expresses a maximin ranking of the alternatives by stating preferences that are based on his least preferred position in each alternative.

The answer, alas, is in the negative. Consider the preferences of table 8.1. In alternative a, all individuals agree that 1 is in the best position and 3 is in the worst; in alternative b, all agree that 2 is in the best position and 1 is in the worst; in alternative c, all agree that 3 is in the best position and 2 is in the worst. Furthermore, the axiom of identity holds. So agreement on all of:

(i)   who is in the best position and who is in the worst in each alternative,
(ii)   which alternative is best and worst for each individual,
(iii)   the use of the maximin principle to derive preferences between alternatives.

is not sufficient to ensure that majority voting between the alternatives gives no voting cycle.

Table 8.1 Maximin principle and voting cycle

individual	preferences over positions (personalised)
1	$[a,1]P_1[b,2]P_1[a,2]P_1[b,3]P_1[c,3]P_1[c,1]P_1[a,3]P_1[b,1]P_1[c,2]$
2	$[b,2]P_2[b,3]P_2[c,3]P_2[a,1]P_2[c,1]P_2[a,2]P_2[b,1]P_2[c,2]P_2[a,3]$
3	$[c,3]P_3[a,1]P_3[c,1]P_3[b,2]P_3[a,2]P_3[b,3]P_3[c,2]P_3[a,3]P_3[b,1]$

9

Utilitarian judgements

To those brought up in the traditions of moral philosophy, or indeed of practical welfare economics, it may seem strange that we have yet to discuss utilitarianism. The idea that we translate 'the greatest good of the greatest number' into the maximisation of the sum of individuals' utilities is of long-standing and deep significance in moral philosophy. Many theorems in welfare economics are based on the maximisation of 'social utility' – but utilitarianism expressed in this way is an uncomfortable doctrine for many social choice theorists because it requires both that we can **measure** individuals' utilities in some meaningful way, and that we can **compare** one person's utility with another's so that, having compared them, we can add them together. In the jargon, the standard utilitarian argument requires both **measurability** and **comparability**.

In chapter 2 we noted that we could use utility statements to replace those involving preference and indifference: instead of saying that i prefers a to b, we could say that i gets more utility from a than he gets from b. We did not do this partly because talking of the utility of an alternative leads to potential misunderstandings. When all we know is an individual's order of preference, we must not be misled into thinking that there is any greater significance in the extent by which the utility of a exceeds that of b: the statement that 'i gets twice as much utility from a as from b' has no more meaning than 'i prefers a to b'. The purpose of this chapter is to examine the ways in which individuals' statements of utility might mean more than order-of-preference statements, and how it may be possible to use these to make social choices or judgements.

9.1 Utility functions

The alternative representation of order-of-preference information as an **ordinal utility function** assigns a number to each alternative. This number is the utility of that alternative, and a more preferred alternative has a higher utility. There is an infinity of ordinal utility functions that can be used to represent a given preference ordering R_i. If i's preferences are consistent with:

$$u_i(a) = 1, u_i(b) = 2 \text{ and } u_i(c) = 3$$

(so that cP_ibP_ia), they are also consistent with:

$$v_i(a) = -7, v_i(b) = 24, v_i(c) = 235$$

Technically any **increasing transformation** of one ordinal utility function generates another ordinal utility function that represents the same order of preference. An increasing transformation preserves the order of the preferences – but not necessarily any numerical differences between or ratios of the utility numbers. In the above example,

$$v_i(x) = (u_i(x))^5 - 8 \text{ for each } x$$

which is an increasing transformation (an increase in u_i always leads to an increase in v_i). Note that the apparent information that y gives twice as much utility as x when function u_i is used is not preserved when v_i is used: for example, if $u_i(x) = 2$ and $u_i(y) = 4$, then $v_i(x) = 24$ and $v_i(y) = 1016$. Only the order of the alternatives is important when we use a utility function of this kind, and only the order is preserved when we use an increasing transformation.

Cardinal utility

The statement:

$$u_i(a) = 6, u_i(b) = 12, u_i(c) = 42$$

could mean more than cP_ibP_ia. The numerical information could imply at least four other statements:

(i) i gets 6 units of utility from a, 12 from b and 42 from c.

(ii) i gets twice as many units of utility from b as from a, and seven times as many from c than from a.

(iii) i gets 6 more units of utility from b than from a, and 36 more from c than from a.

(iv)   the difference $u_i(c) - u_i(a)$ is 6 times the difference $u_i(b) - u_i(a)$.

These interpretations are not the same because each is preserved by different changes in the utility function:

(i)   Is true only for the given numbers.

(ii)   Remains true if there are proportional changes in the units used to measure utility such as $v_i(a) = 3$, $v_i(b) = 6$, $v_i(c) = 21$, so that $v_i = u_i/2$.

(iii) Remains true if there are shifts in the origin of the scale used for measuring utility, but not for changes in the units, such as $v_i(a) = 53$, $v_i(b) = 59$, $v_i(c) = 89$, so that $v_i = u_i + 47$.

(iv)   Remains true if there are changes in the origin and changes in the units, such as $v_i(a) = -2$, $v_i(b) = 1$, $v_i(c) = 16$, so that $v_i = -5 + u_i/2$.

From a technical point of view, these alternative interpretations of the statement are reflected in the transformations of the utility function that preserve the information that the utility functions are intended to convey. The utility function v_i is a **positive linear transformation** of u_i if:

$$v_i = \alpha + \beta u_i$$

(where α is any number, β is any positive number).

(i)   To preserve the information in the first interpretation, α must be zero and β must be 1: that is, no changes can be allowed.

(ii)   To preserve the information in the second interpretation, α must be zero, and β can be any positive real number (0.5 in the example).

(iii) To preserve the information in the third interpretation, α can be any number, and β must equal one (in the example, $\alpha = 47$).

(iv)   Any positive linear transformation preserves information in the fourth interpretation (in the example given, $\alpha = -5$, $\beta = 0.5$).

We can contrast these restrictions to linear transformations with the fact that the ordinal interpretation of a utility function is preserved by any positive transformation – linear or non-linear – that keeps the utility numbers in the same order.

9.2 von Neumann – Morgenstern utility

One solution to the problem of measuring an individual's utility was put forward by von Neumann and Morgenstern (1944) in their work on the theory of games. The **von Neumann – Morgenstern (vN – M) utility index** is based on the assumption that an individual can make statements of preference between alternatives and **lotteries** of alternatives. A lottery between alternatives x and y is described by a probability p that x will occur and a corresponding probability $1 - p$ that y will occur. We name such a lottery $L(x,p; y,1 - p)$. For example, tossing a fair coin is L(heads, 0.5; tails, 0.5). Probabilities are always expressed as numbers between 0 (no chance of getting the alternative) and 1 (certainly getting the alternative). We refer also to lotteries between more than two alternatives such as $L(a,p; b,q; c,1 - p - q)$, in which the probability of getting a is p, the probability of getting b is q, and that of getting c is $1 - p - q$. The total of the probabilities in a lottery must always be 1.

A vN−M utility index is constructed as follows: the individual names his most preferred alternative and least preferred alternative (or chooses one of each if several tie): suppose that these are a and z respectively. We choose two numbers $u_i(a)$ and $u_i(z)$ that determine his highest and lowest utilities. We can choose $u_i(a)$ and $u_i(z)$ to be any numbers, provided that $u_i(a)$ exceeds $u_i(z)$ to reflect the fact that i prefers a to z.

Consider an alternative b for which aP_ibP_iz. In terms of lotteries, i prefers b to the lottery $L(a,0; z,1)$ (that is, certainly getting z), and i prefers $L(a,1; z,0)$ (that is, certainly getting a) to b. Von Neumann and Morgenstern presume that, at some intermediate probability p, i is indifferent between b and $L(a,p; z,1 - p)$: he is indifferent between the certain prospect of b, and the uncertain prospect of getting either a or z, with probabilities p and $1 - p$ respectively. Then the vN – M utility of b is defined as

$$u_i(b) = pu_i(a) + (1 - p)u_i(z)$$

This procedure can be followed for each alternative, giving a **von Neumann – Morgenstern utility function**.

The vN – M utility function described above has a range from $u_i(z)$ to $u_i(a)$. There are other vN – M utility functions that represent the same preferences, but with different ranges, and different utility units: these are found by changing the arbitrarily chosen values of $u_i(a)$ and $u_i(z)$. Any two vN – M functions that represent the same preferences are related by a positive linear transformation as the following example shows. Suppose that a is the best alternative and z is the worst, and that $bI_iL(a,p; z,1 - p)$. Then we can define two utility functions u_i and v_i with:

$$u_i(a) = 100, u_i(z) = 40$$
$$v_i(a) = 60, v_i(z) = 6$$

so that:

$$u_i(b) = p.100 + (1-p).40 = 40 + 60p$$
$$v_i(b) = p.60 + (1-p).6 = 6 + 54p$$

Some algebra gives:

$$v_i(b) = -30 + 0.9u_i(b)$$

So:

$$v_i = \alpha + ßu_i \text{ where } \alpha = -30 \text{ and } ß = 0.9.$$

9.3 Measurability without comparability

Social choice involves aggregating different individuals' preferences – and in a utilitarian framework this requires that we can measure utilities in units that are comparable between individuals. There are two ingredients of utilitarian judgements: comparability and measurability, and, if both ingredients are present, we can make utilitarian judgements. What happens if one is present and one is absent? Can we move any distance from the problems raised by Arrow's theorem if we assume that each individual's utility can be measured (using a vN – M utility function, for example) even though it is not possible to compare the units in which different individuals' utilities are measured. Does the extra information available in the form of cardinal utilities (compared to Arrow's use of ordinal preferences) avoid Arrow's inevitable dictator?

Suppose that individual i has preferences which can be represented by utility function u_i, and that can be equally represented by any positive linear transformation of u_i (as in the vN – M method). To mirror Arrow's condition of unrestricted preferences, we assume that the social choice rule gives transitive social preferences whatever utilities each individual may express; we call this condition **unrestricted utilities**. Further, the condition of **independence of positive linear transformations** requires that the social choice from any set of alternatives should be unchanged if each individual's utility function u_i is replaced by a positive linear transformation v_i, where:

$$v_i = \alpha_i + ß_iu_i \text{ and } ß_i > 0$$

Finally, we presume that the social choice rule uses <u>only</u> information on the utilities of the alternatives: if we consider two different utility functions representing different preferences (so that u_i and v_i are not related by a positive linear transformation) for each individual, and if for alternatives a and b, $u_i(a) = v_i(a)$ and $u_i(b) = v_i(b)$ for every individual, then the social choice rule gives the same social preference between a and b for the two sets of utility functions. This is the **independence** condition translated into utility terms. Then Arrow's theorem can be used to show:

Theorem 9.1 There is a dictator if a social choice rule defines complete and transitive social preferences and satisfies
  unrestricted utilities
  weak Pareto
  independence of positive linear transformations
  independence

The proof simply requires that we can translate its conditions into those of Arrow's theorem – and, in particular, that Arrow's independence condition holds. Suppose that, for each individual the utility functions u_i and v_i give the same order of preference between alternatives a and b. For each individual we can define a third utility function w_i which gives the same numerical utilities as v_i for a and b, and which is a positive linear transformation of u_i. For example, suppose that there are four alternatives and for some individual i:

$$u_i(a) = 10, \ u_i(b) = 7, \ u_i(c) = 2 \ u_i(d) = 0$$
$$v_i(a) = 15, \ v_i(b) = 6, \ v_i(c) = 20, \ v_i(d) = 9$$

Both u_i and v_i place a and b in the same order. Then construct

$$w_i = -15 + 3u_i$$

so that w_i is a positive linear transformation of u_i and $w_i(a) = v_i(a)$ and $w_i(b) = v_i(b)$

$$w_i(a) = 15, \ w_i(b) = 6, \ w_i(c) = -9, \ w_i(d) = -15.$$

If we construct such a w_i for each individual, the independence condition implies that the utilities (w_i) and (v_i) must give the same social preference between a and b, and independence of positive linear transformations implies that (u_i) and (w_i) must give the same social preference between a and b. So, if no individual changes his order of preference between two alternatives (even if he changes his utility function), there can be no change in social preferences – the pairwise independence condition holds. All the other conditions needed in Arrow's theorem plainly hold too, and so dictatorship is inevitable.

So we do not escape from Arrow's dictatorship by using cardinal, but non-comparable, utility information about preferences. We can do so if we were able to use comparable, measurable utilities which we can add together because then each person has similar influence on the social choice, and so no-one is a dictator. There seems to be no satisfactory way of finding such utilities.

9.4 Utilitarianism and justice

The general use of cardinal utilities involves difficulties of comparison and measurement, but it is possible to use vN – M utilities in an impersonal framework where a single individual is making a judgement (see section 8.1). If an individual has preferences over positions in alternatives, and wants to use a theory of justice that does not put particular weight on his own position in each alternative, he might construct a vN – M utility function to give the utilities of each position, and then use this to derive a utilitarian judgement of the alternatives. Suppose that there are three alternatives (a,b,c) and three positions $(1,2,3)$ and i's preferences are as in table 9.1. The best position is $[a,1]$, the worst is $[b,3]$. Suppose then that, by constructing the lotteries needed for the vN – M function, we discover that i is indifferent between $[b,1]$ and $L([a,1],0.8;[b,3],0.2)$.

Similarly, $[a,2]I_iL([a,1],0.7;[b,3],0.3)$, and so on, using the probabilities listed in table 9.1.

Table 9.1 Probabilities and alternative vN–M functions

preferences	probability	vN – M(1) u_i	vN – M(2) v_i
$[a,1]P_i$	1	100	212
$[b,1]P_i$	0.8	80	176
$[a,2]P_i$	0.7	70	158
$[c,1]P_i$	0.64	64	147.2
$[a,3]P_i$	0.55	55	131
$[c,2]I_i[c,3]P_i$	0.4	40	104
$[b,2]P_i$	0.1	10	50
$[b,3]$	0	0	32

Consider alternative a: in an impersonal theory, i believes that he has an equal chance of holding each of $[a,1]$, $[a,2]$ and $[a,3]$ so that he wants to give these three positions equal weight in his judgement of a. Given an equal chance of getting $[a,1]$, $[a,2]$ and $[a,3]$, alternative a is equivalent to a lottery $L_0 = L([a,1],\frac{1}{3}; [a,2],\frac{1}{3}; [a,3],\frac{1}{3})$. Individual i is indifferent between $[a,2]$ and $L_1 = L([a,1],0.7; [b,3],0.3)$; and i is indifferent between $[a,3]$ and $L_2 = L([a,1],0.55; [b,3],0.45)$. So L_0 is equivalent to $L([a,1],\frac{1}{3}; L_1,\frac{1}{3}; L_2,\frac{1}{3})$, which is a lottery in which there are three possible 'prizes', with equal probabilities:

(i) first prize is $[a,1]$,
(ii) second prize is entry in a lottery L_1 in which $[a,1]$ has a probability of 0.7 and $[b,3]$ has a probability of 0.3,
(iii) third prize is entry in a lottery L_2 in which $[a,1]$ has a probability of 0.55 and $[b,3]$ has a probability of 0.45.

So the overall probability of getting $[a,1]$ in lottery L_0 is:

$$\tfrac{1}{3} + (\tfrac{1}{3})\text{x}0.7 + (\tfrac{1}{3}) \times 0.55 = 0.75.$$

Thus individual i is indifferent between $L([a,1], 0.75; [b,3], 0.25)$ and alternative a. Similarly it is possible to show that $bI_iL([a,1], 0.3; [b,3], 0.7)$ and $cI_iL([a,1], 0.48; [b,3], 0.52)$.

We can use the vN – M method to find the utilities of each position if we assign arbitrary levels of utility to the best outcome $[a,1]$ and the worst $[b,3]$. The final two columns of table 9.1 do this; first with $u_i[a,1] = 100$ and $u_i[b,3] = 0$, and second with $v_i[a,1] = 212$ and $v_i[b,3] = 32$. Using u_i, the average utility of the three positions in alternative a is:

$$(\tfrac{1}{3}) [100 + 70 + 55] = 75$$

The average utility of the three positions in alternative b is:

$$(\tfrac{1}{3}) [80 + 10 + 0] = 30$$

The average utility of the three positions in alternative c is:

$$(\tfrac{1}{3}) [64 + 40 + 40] = 48$$

These utilities are obviously linearly related to the probabilities in the lotteries to which a, b and c are indifferent:

$$u_i(a) = 100 \times 0.75, \; u_i(b) = 100 \text{ x } 0.3, \; u_i(c) = 100 \times 0.48$$

The same conclusion holds using v_i. The average utility of the three positions in alternative a is:

$$(\tfrac{1}{3}) [212 + 158 + 131] = 167$$

The average utility of the three positions in alternative b is:

$$(\tfrac{1}{3}) [176 + 50 + 32] = 86$$

The average utility of the three positions in alternative c is:

$(\frac{1}{3})$ [147.2 + 104 + 104] = 118.4

Then:

$$v_i(a) = 32 + 180 \times 0.75$$
$$v_i(b) = 32 + 180 \times 0.3$$
$$v_i(c) = 32 + 180 \times 0.48$$

Once again the utilities are linearly related to the probabilities.

This analysis implies that, if we use vN – M method to give utilities of each position, and the individual judges each alternative by assuming that he has an equal probability of occupying any position, then we can construct utilities of the alternatives (we can construct these for any arbitrary utilities of the best and worst positions as table 9.1 shows). Individual i can then use these to judge the alternatives, and come up with his own ordering of the alternatives. Note that this is an impersonal form of utilitarianism: the preferences involved are those of one individual considering each possible position. Thus there is no need to try to add together different individuals' utilities, so that the question of comparability does not arise.

There are some assumptions about preferences hidden in this derivation of the utilitarian principle of justice. First, we have assumed that i regards $L([a,1], \frac{1}{3}; [a,2], \frac{1}{3}; [a,3], \frac{1}{3})$ as equivalent to $L([a,1], \frac{1}{3}; L_1, \frac{1}{3}; L_2, \frac{1}{3})$.

The first is a lottery with three possible outcomes, each of which is a position: the second is a lottery with three outcomes and the same probabilities, but two of these outcomes are themselves lotteries. Is it reasonable to suppose that the individual's preference remains unaffected if we replace a non-probabilistic outcome with a lottery, even if the individual is indifferent between the non-probabilistic outcome and the lottery? If you are indifferent between receiving £40 and $L(£100, \frac{1}{3}; £0, \frac{2}{3})$, are you indifferent between two lotteries that are otherwise identical, but one of which has £40 as a prize and one of which has $L(£100, \frac{1}{3}; £0, \frac{2}{3})$ as a prize? This is an empirical question whose answer affects the plausibility of this impersonal utilitarian principle of justice.

The second point to note is that the individual making the judgement interprets 'impersonality' as implying that he should give equal weight to each of the possible positions within each alternative. This contrasts (not necessarily unfavourably) with Rawls' maximin criterion which judges each alternative according to the worst position in it. Using Rawls' maximin, we can still derive utilities for each alternative from the vN – M functions: using u_i, the utilities of a, b and c would be 55, 40, 0; using v_i they would be 131, 104, 32. However, they are not utilitarian in the sense that they are related to the utilities that each person gets in a, b and c respectively (in our example, maximin gives a different ordering of the alternatives to the average utility method).

9.5 Utilitarianism and Arrow's theorem

For most of this book, we have avoided utilitarianism as a possible way out from the problems raised by Arrow's theorem and its derivatives. We have done this because there seemed to be difficulties with measuring and comparing individual utilities. Now that we have found a way of deriving and using vN – M utilities, it is fair to ask whether this approach in fact helps to meet difficulties raised in previous chapters.

Some, such as Harsanyi (1955) would argue that this use of von Neumann – Morgenstern utility functions to make social choices has saved at least ethical theory from Arrow's inevitable dictator. These supporters argue that each person ought to give equal weight to the positions of every individual, and as long as the behavioural assumptions on the combination of lotteries is valid, then the utilitarian judgements are possible.

In discussing utilitarianism in the context of Arrow's theorem we must recognise first that the use of lotteries to derive vN – M utilities implies impersonality: to create a lottery, an individual must decide whether he prefers the certainty of being in position $[b,2]$ to a lottery between $[a,1]$ or $[c,3]$. In each case, he has to imagine himself in each of the positions – he might 'win' either of the lottery outcomes as the 'prize'. It is impossible to use this method except in an impersonal context. If j knew that individual i would occupy $[a,2]$ in alternative a and $[b,3]$ in alternative b, he could not derive probabilities using i's preferences because he has no way of comparing i's intensity of preference with his own. Individual j can only use his own preferences to derive the vN – M lottery probabilities. For example, suppose that j is a smoker and i is a non-smoker, and the positions relate to possibilities of working in rooms where smoking is banned. Individual j may know that i prefers to work in a smoke-free environment, but it is difficult to argue that j can estimate the probabilities that effectively define i's intensity of preference for this; j could use i's preferences to determine his own ordering of the positions using the liberal argument that i's preferences should determine where i works, but j cannot use i's preferences to determine cardinal utilities.

This method of making utilitarian judgements does not resolve the problem of reconciling the preferences of different individuals in a personal context: it does not remove the problems of Arrow's theorem that arise when individuals have suitably diverse preferences. Theorem 9.1 demonstrates that the ability to measure utilities using the vN – M method does not avoid dictatorship when preferences diverge and when we accept that we have no satisfactory basis for comparing the utilities of different individuals.

This example implies that the vN – M approach is of limited use, but it may be applicable in some circumstances. It is conventionally assumed in economics that people have preferences (or utilities) over income levels including those quite different from their own. If this is so, people can make the judgements needed to construct vN – M utilities of positions which are described by income levels. Then an individual who is very averse to the risk of being very poor would give low utilities to positions with low incomes, and would give greater total utilities to even distributions of a given income than to very unequal distributions.

In sum, there are some contexts where judgements might be made using vN – M utilities but in many circumstances the problems of Arrow's theorem and its extensions and the difficulties involved in liberalism and justice remain.

Bibliography

Arrow, K.J. (1950). A Difficulty in the Concept of Social Welfare. *Journal of Political Economy*. **58**, 328–46

(1951). *Social Choice and Individual Values*. Cowles Foundation Monograph 12. New York: John Wiley

(1984). *Social Choice and Justice*. Volume 1 in the collected papers of Kenneth J. Arrow. Oxford: Basil Blackwell

Barbera, S. (1976). Manipulation of Social Decision Mechanisms. *Journal of Economic Theory*. **76**, 266–78

Bartholdi, J.J., Tovey, C.A. and Trick, M.A. (1989). The Computational Difficulty of Manipulating an Election. *Social Choice and Welfare*. **6**, 227–41

Bergson, A. (1938).A Reformulation of Certain Aspects of Welfare Economics. *Quarterly Journal of Economics*. **52**, 310–34

Black, D. (1948). On the Rationale of Group Decision – Making. *Journal of Political Economy*. **56**, 23–34

(1958). *The Theory of Committees and Elections*. Cambridge: Cambridge University Press

Blau, J.H. (1957). The Existence of a Social Welfare Function. *Econometrica*. **25**, 302–13

(1975). Liberal Values and Independence. *Review of Economic Studies*. **42**, 395–401

Craven, J. (1971). Majority Voting and Social Choice. *Review of Economic Studies*. **38**, 265–7

(1983). Social Choice and Telling the Truth. *Journal of Public Economics*. **21**, 359–75

(1984). *Proportional Representation in Single Member Constituencies*. University of Kent at Canterbury

(1988). Extended Majority Rule and Acyclic Social Preferences. University of Kent at Canterbury: *Studies in Economics*. **88/2**

Dasgupta, P.S. Hammond, P.J. and Maskin, E.S. (1979). The Implementation of Social Choice Rules: Some General Results on Incentive Compatibility. *Review of Economic Studies.* **46**, 185–216

de Borda, J – C. (1781). Mémoire sur les élections au scrutin. *Mémoires de l'Académie Royale des Sciences.* 657–65 (for a translation, see A. de Grazia (1953). *Isis.* **44** , 42–51)

de Condorcet, Marquis. (1785). *Essai sur l'Application de l'Analyse à la Probabilité des Décisions Rendues à la Pluralité des Voix.* Paris

Debreu, G. (1959). *The Theory of Value.* New York: Wiley

Denicolò, V. (1987). Some Further Results on Nonbinary Social Choice. *Social Choice and Welfare.* **4**, 277–85

Dodgson, C.L. (1876). *A Method of Taking Votes on More Than Two Issues.* Oxford: Clarendon Press

Dummett, M. (1984). *Voting Procedures.* Oxford: Oxford University Press

Gibbard, A. (1969). *Social Choice and the Arrow Conditions.* Unpublished

(1973). Manipulation of Voting Schemes: A General Result. *Econometrica.* **41**, 587–601

(1974). A Pareto – Consistent Libertarian Claim. *Journal of Economic Theory.* **7**, 388–410

Guha, A.S. (1972). Monotonicity, Neutrality, and the Right of Veto. *Econometrica.* **40**, 821–6

Hammond, P.J. (1976). Equity, Arrow's Conditions and Rawls' Difference Principle. *Econometrica.* **44**, 793–804

Harsanyi, J.C. (1955). Cardinal Welfare, Individualist Ethics and Interpersonal Comparisons of Utility. *Journal of Political Economy.* **61**, 309–21

Hicks, J.R. (1939). *Value and Capital.* OxfordClarendon Press

Intriligator, M.D. (1973). A Probabilistic Model of Social Choice. *Review of Economic Studies.* **40**, 553–60

Kaldor, N. (1939). Welfare Propositions in Economics. *Economic Journal.* **49**, 549–52

Kemp, M.C. and Ng, Y.K. (1976). On the Existence of Social Welfare Functions, Social Orderings and Social Decision Functions. *Economica.* **43**, 59–66

MacKay, A.F. (1980). *Arrow's Theorem: the Paradox of Social Choice.* New Haven and London: Yale University Press

Mas-Colell, A. and Sonnenschein, H. (1972). General Possibility Theorems for Group Decisions. *Review of Economic Studies.* **39**, 185–92

May, K.O. (1952). A Set of Independent, Necessary and Sufficient Conditions for Simple Majority Decision. *Econometrica.* **20**, 680–4

Nanson, E.J. (1882). Methods of Election. *Transactions and Proceedings of the Royal Society of Victoria.* **19**, 197–240

Newland, R.A. (1982). *Comparative Electoral Systems.* London: The Arthur McDougall Fund; Electoral Reform Society

Parks, R.P. (1976). An Impossibility theorem for Fixed Preferences: A Dictatorial Bergson – Samuelson Welfare Function. *Review of Economic Studies.* **43**, 447–50

Pattanaik, P.K. (1978). *Strategy and Group Choice*. Amsterdam: North-Holland

Pearce, D.W. (1971). *Cost – Benefit Analysis*. London: Macmillan

Plott, C.R. (1973). Path Independence, Rationality, and Social Choice. *Econometrica*. **41**, 1075–91

Rawls, J. (1971). *A Theory of Justice*. Cambridge, Mass.: Harvard University Press

Samuelson, P.A. (1947). *Foundations of Economic Analysis*. Cambridge, Mass.: Harvard University Press

(1977). Reaffirming the Existence of Reasonable Bergson – Samuelson Social Welfare Functions. *Economica*. **44**, 81–8

Satterthwaite, M.A. (1975). Strategy – proofness and Arrow's Conditions. *Journal of Economic Theory*. **10**, 187–217

Scitovsky, T. (1941). A Note on Welfare Propositions in Economics. *Review of Economic Studies*. **9**, 77–88

Sen, A.K. (1969). Quasitransitivity, Rational Choice and Collective Decisions. *Review of Economic Studies*. **36**, 381–93

(1970a). *Collective Choice and Social Welfare*. Edinburgh: Oliver and Boyd

(1970b). The Impossibility of a Paretian Liberal. *Journal of Political Economy*. **78**, 152–7

(1971). Choice Functions and Revealed Preference. *Review of Economic Studies*. **38**, 307–17

(1976). Liberty, Unanimity and Rights. *Economica*. **43**, 217–45

(1977a). Social Choice Theory, a Re-examination. *Econometrica*. **45**, 53–89

(1977b). On Weights and Measures: Informational Constraints in Social Welfare Analysis. *Econometrica*. **45**, 1539–72

(1979). Personal Utilities and Public Judgements: or What's Wrong with Welfare Economics? *Economic Journal*. **89**, 537–58

(1982). *Choice, Measurement and Welfare*. Oxford: Basil Blackwell

Sen, A.K. and Pattanaik, P.K. (1969). Necessary and Sufficient Conditions for Rational Choices under Majority Decision. *Journal of Economic Theory*. **1**, 178–202

Smith, A. (1776). *An Enquiry into the Nature and Causes of the Wealth of Nations*. Harmondsworth: Penguin (1970 paperback edition)

Sugden, R. (1981). *The Political Economy of Public Choice*. Oxford: Martin Robertson

Suppes, P. (1966). Some Formal Models of Grading Principles. *Synthese*. **6**, 284–306

Suzumura, K. (1978). On the Consistency of Libertarian Claims. *Review of Economic Studies*. **45**, 329–42

(1983). *Rational Choice, Collective Decisions and Social Welfare*. Cambridge: Cambridge University Press

Varian, H. (1987). *Intermediate Microeconomics*. London: Norton

Vickrey, W. (1960). Utility, Strategy and Social Decision Rules. *Quarterly Journal of Economics*. **74**, 507–35

von Neumann, J. and Morgenstern, O. (1944). *Theory of Games and Economic Behaviour*. Princeton: Princeton University Press

Wriglesworth, J. (1985). *Libertarian Conflicts in Social Choice*. Cambridge: Cambridge University Press

Index